STUDENT IMPACT

MW01105916

A LIFELONG CALLING

TWELVE LESSONS THAT WILL IMPACT THE WORLD

VOLUME FOUR

Small Group

RESOURCES

BO BOSHERS

Erin Frazier and Tricia Murphy

ZondervanPublishingHouse
Grand Rapids, Michigan

A Division of HarperCollinsPublishers

WILLOW CREEK
RESOURCES

I would like to dedicate this curriculum to each of you with a shepherd's heart who has been called by God to serve high school students. I pray that the small groups on these pages will be a powerful resource for gathering students together and putting them on the path to becoming fully devoted followers of Christ. May God richly bless you for following the call He's placed on your heart to impact the lives of students … you are making a difference.

Serving together, one life at a time,
Bo

A Lifelong Calling © 1997 by The Willow Creek Association

Requests for information should be addressed to:
ZondervanPublishingHouse
Grand Rapids, Michigan 49530

ISBN: 0–310–20128–4

Interior design by Jack Rogers

Printed in the United States of America

98 99 00 01 02 03 04 /❖ ML/ 10 9 8 7 6 5 4

CONTENTS

ACKNOWLEDGMENTS

I would like to recognize and express my thanks to those who were instrumental in making this project happen.

To Tricia Murphy, who used her creativity, devotion, and desire to capture God's Truth for the result of moving students practically to find the love of Christ. Thank you for your friendship and sensitivity.

To Troy Murphy, my lifelong friend, who used his artistic gifts to help create the right format for sharing this resource. Thank you for your devotion to this project; I love running the race with you.

To Erin Frazier, who joined the team through her willingness to take a step of adventure in using her gift of writing. Thank you for your contribution and promptness; I hope there are more projects for us to do together in the future.

To Lynette Rubin, my friend and assistant, for her availability, support, and willingness to adjust when I needed it. I could not have done this without you.

To Dave Lambert, Rachel Boers, Jane Vogel, and their teams at Zondervan, who gave us understanding, support, patience, and direction in developing this project. Thank you for your time and energy.

And to the Willow Creek Association team, for the many people who were involved in making this desire for small group curriculum a reality. Thank you for the privilege of doing this project with you. Together we have all seen a dream come true.

Introduction

You are holding in your hands an exciting tool! It's not every day that you can find a tool that will:
   • assist you in touching the lives of high school students with whom you are involved—as a full-time, part-time, or volunteer youth leader;
   • equip you to talk to your students in ways that will allow them to experience God in more intimate ways;
   • change the way you develop small groups in your student ministry.
   Walk through the next few pages and catch the vision for this tool that will help you make a difference in the lives of high school students.

The next few pages are devoted to sharing a vision for small groups in student ministry. You will discover how small groups can most effectively be used to bring about life changes and specifically how to implement small groups using the experiences in this book. Take plenty of time to reflect on the impact these opportunities for community and growth can have on the students whose lives you influence.

WHY SMALL GROUPS?
Change—The Purpose of Small Groups
Small groups are essential to the development of spiritual life in those who want to be fully devoted followers of Christ. They are essential because community, growth, sharing, and discipleship happen in the context of a group. In Student Impact, the high school ministry of Willow Creek Community Church in Barrington, Illinois, we refer to our small groups as D-Teams (with the "D" representing the Greek word *Delta*, meaning "change.") Our mission is simply to turn irreligious high school students into fully devoted followers of Christ.

   To accomplish this mission, Student Impact is based on a seven-step strategy. Everything we do fits into this strategy:

1. Integrity Friendship
   The process begins as we challenge our core students to build "relational bridges" with their non-Christian friends.

2. Verbal Witness
   After students have built credible friendships with their non-Christian friends, we teach them to look for opportunities to explain and discuss their relationship with Christ.

3. Supplemental Witness: Providing a Service for Seekers
   Student Impact, our service for seekers, is designed to nurture students' spiritual interest by introducing them to the message of Christ in a contemporary and relevant way. Impact is intended to be used as a tool by our core in reaching their non-Christian friends by supplementing their ongoing witness.

4. Spiritual Challenge
   At this stage of their friendship, we teach our core students to ask pointed questions that intentionally challenge their friends to consider the claims of Christ. We believe that once a seeker has spent time listening to God's Word and observing fully devoted Christian students, he will discover through the conviction of the Holy Spirit his need for a personal relationship with Jesus Christ.

5. Integration into the Body

   Student Insight, our worship service for believers, is designed to mature the believer on the trek toward full devotion to Christ. Insight provides believers with an opportunity to participate in corporate worship and to listen to expository Bible teaching.

6. Discipleship Through Small Groups

   Small groups provide a discipleship atmosphere. From this small group comes accountability, encouragement, and support, as well as Biblical teaching through learning experiences.

7. Ownership

   At this stage of spiritual development, students are taking an active role in service within the church. Through both financial giving and using their spiritual gifts, they are owning their part of the Lord's work. A student now steps forward and takes the role of evangelist within his own circle of influence and thus begins a third spiritual generation. This occurs as he takes his non-Christian friends through the same seven steps he traveled.

The vision of Student Impact is to create a unique community of students and leaders committed to letting God

- change their lives;
- change their friends' lives;
- build the church; and
- impact the world.

The four volumes of small group experiences, *Walking with Christ, Compassion for Lost People, Learning to Serve,* and *A Lifelong Calling,* are written with these four values (we call them "waves" of ministry) in mind. This book of experiences focuses on the fourth wave of life change: outreach to the world. As a student walks the road of fully devoted followership, he or she will inevitably be drawn to impact the world for Christ. This volume will assist you in sharing the vision for making a difference around the world.

For a fuller development of how small groups fit into the vision and mission of student ministry, see *Student Ministry for the 21st Century: Transforming Your Youth Group into a Vital Student Ministry* by Bo Boshers with Kim Anderson (Zondervan, 1997).

Authenticity—Leading by Example

As the leader of small group life, your role is not only to teach the Word of God, but to be an example to your students. It's more than talking. It's living in the moment with students, thinking the way they think, asking questions that allow them to reflect on their world, creating an environment that provides opportunities for uninterrupted community and soul-searching. These moments are about helping students take the time to look at Christ and grow to be more like Him. It's about life change.

In Student Impact, D-Teams meet every other week. But our walk with Christ is lived out daily. Today's students are looking for leaders who live authentic lives in Christ. As a leader, you not only facilitate the D-Team experiences, but you work to help students view the world from God's perspective each day. The greatest lesson students learn is not from these materials but from your life. This can happen only through your commitment of time, prayer, and preparation. The D-Team experiences in this book will serve as the basis for group interaction, but the key to fully devoted followership is allowing God to work through you so that students experience Him.

If you're unfamiliar with the D-Team format, take a few minutes to read the following overview.

HOW TO USE THIS BOOK

For each small group meeting, you'll find Leader's Notes that will guide you through your preparation and actual leading of the group experience, and Student Notes that you can photocopy and distribute to your students to use during your time together. The Student Notes are designed so that you can photocopy the two pages back-to-back, then fold them to form a four-page booklet that your students can slip easily into their Bibles. (You'll notice that the page numbers on the Student Notes look out of order when they are unassembled.) Encourage your students to take their notes home, perhaps filing them in a notebook or binder, so they can look back at what they've learned throughout their small group experiences.

The Leader's Notes contain all the information in the Student Notes plus the following features to help you prepare and lead your students.

Unit Introduction

Each unit begins with an introduction that includes the Leader Focus and Big Picture. The Leader Focus will help you begin thinking about the unit theme from a new perspective. In the Big Picture, you'll find a brief description of the values and objectives for each unit as well as the D-Team experiences themselves. You'll also get your first look at the Unit Memory Verse. Each unit builds on the one before, but you can also use the units independently if that's more appropriate for your time frame or the needs of your particular students. You'll notice that the lessons within each unit are numbered independent of the other units to give you this flexibility.

Before the D-Team Experience

Each session has an easy-to-use summary outline that will help you see the D-Team experience at a glance.

• *Leader Devotion*—To impact students at the deepest level, there can be no mistaking the value of a leader's personal authenticity. The heart of the leader is key. This section will challenge you to recall personal experiences and gain new insights that you can share with your students. This mini-devotion will prepare you for the role of leadership.

• *Student Focus*—This section provides the leader with the rationale for the D-Team experience. It provides clarification on what a student can expect if he or she is committed to this experience and the truths to be learned. It may also provide an opening discussion question.

• *Unit Memory Verse*—Only four memory verses appear in each volume. When students focus on memorizing one verse per unit, they will truly have ownership of that verse and can apply it to their lives on a daily basis.

• *Practical Impact*—We believe students learn best when they experience God's truth, not just talk about it. Each Practical Impact section outlines ways for students not only to hear the Word of God, but to experience it.

• *Materials Needed*—Here you will find a list of everything you need to bring to the D-Team experience. Student Notes are provided for each D-Team experience and can be duplicated back-to-back for your D-Team members. Encourage your students to keep these notes in a binder so they can look back on what they've learned.

• *Special Preparation*—In this section, you will find detailed instructions to help you prepare for your D-Team experience. Phone contacts, letters, reproducible handouts, suggestions about advance phone contacts and letters, and other ideas for resources will help ensure that your D-Team experience goes smoothly.

• *Environment*—Because students are sometimes more able to freely experience God outside the context of four walls, each D-Team experience offers two options. Option 1 works in any setting, while Option 2 moves the experience outside a normal meeting room to an environment that has been created especially for the D-Team. Option 2 takes time and thought on the part of the leader, but it can set up a D-Team experience in a very powerful way. Explore your options. Figure out what freedom you have in this area. Depending on the size or structure of your student ministry, the environment can be established in different ways. If a large number of students meet together before they divide into different D-Teams, a master teacher approach can help to establish the environment by "painting a picture," then dismissing students.

Leading the D-Team Experience (60 min.)

Your entire D-Team experience should last approximately 60 minutes. It's divided into four sections: Get Started (5 minutes), The Experience (40 minutes), Reflection (5 minutes), and Make an Impact (10 minutes). Questions and Scriptures that are ***bold-face and italic*** in your Leader's Notes are duplicated in the Student Notes.

Get Started (5 min.)

During the first five minutes of the first D-Team experience of each unit, you will help your students: preview the objectives of the unit; understand the Unit Memory Verse; spend some time in prayer; and discover what to expect in this D-Team experience. In the next two D-Team experiences of each unit, you will use this time to review assignments and challenges from the previous D-Team experiences, encourage student-led prayer, and share objectives for the new D-Team experience.

The Experience (40 min.)

This forty-minute section is broken down into several steps to help you lead the experience. This is the practical work and discussion section for the students. You'll find step-by-step instructions along with discussion questions, Bible study, activities, and various practical exercises. Feel free to insert your own thoughts and insights—things God showed you during your Leader Devotion time as well as in your general preparation for the D-Team experience.

Reflection (5 min.)

This five-minute portion of the experience will help your group members solidify the truths they have learned as they reflect individually on the experience. Encourage your D-Team members to truly invest in this section. Model for them the value of reflection as you work through the questions listed here. Don't be afraid of the silence of reflection as opportunities for growth are being formed in students' minds! Model openness in your own personal application, but especially encourage your D-Team members to share their ideas on how to apply the truths in their lives. Use the Summary Statements to reinforce the truths the students have learned.

Make an Impact (10 min.)

During the last ten minutes of your D-Team experience, you have the opportunity to challenge your students to make personal applications of the principles they have experienced. Don't forget to seek God's guidance for each of your students.

- *... In Your Life*—Students like to be challenged. This section allows you to offer some sort of assignment and challenge to your D-Team members. Let them know they have a choice in accepting the challenges. Make it inviting to commit, but not easy. Remind your students that it takes training to develop godly character (1 Tim. 4:7b–8) that will bear fruit.

- *... With Accountability*—In this section, you will encourage each student to choose another person in the D-Team as an accountability partner. Together, they will work on the Unit Memory Verse. In addition, accountability partners will have opportunities to share their responses to assignments and challenges.

- *Prayer*—Be sure to close the D-Team experience in prayer. Model the value of prayer by upholding it before and after each D-Team experience. Invite your students to pray as they are comfortable. Explore this opportunity to pray in community with your D-Team members if you find that they are hesitant to pray aloud. You may ask certain students to pray for specific areas as you sense the development of community and safety.

FOLLOW UP

If you have more than one small group, you can use the Shepherding Summary Form (page XX) to enable communication between D-Team leaders and the ministry director. Duplicate this form and have each D-Team Leader in your student ministry fill it out after each D-Team experience. Simply indicate brief responses to the questions in each section. Over time, this process will assist you in accountability, opportunities for encouragement, record-keeping for D-Team member information, and direction-setting for your student ministry leader.

LEADER FOCUS

Read Isaiah 45:22. This is such a simple statement, yet it is the crux of our faith. If there is one thing we want the world to know, it is that God—and only God—is the answer. In Unit 1 you and your students will be discussing God's plan for the world. Take a moment to read this verse again, and then spend time in prayer for the "ends of the earth."

BIG PICTURE

Unit Overview
In Unit 1 we will be focusing on God's plan for the world by answering three questions: (1) What promise has God made to the world? (2) How should we respond to God's promise? (3) What is God's plan to reach the world?

1. God So Loved the World
During this D-Team experience, your students will discover how much God loves the world by answering three questions:

  Question #1: What is a promise?
  Question #2: What are some of God's promises?
  Question #3: What is the Ultimate Promise?

2. Every Knee Shall Bow
During this D-Team experience, your students will discover two keys to understanding God's love for the world:

  Key #1: Everyone is given the chance to hear God's Truth.
  Key #2: Everyone has an opportunity to accept God's Truth.

3. Impact the World
During this D-Team experience, your students will discover that God's plan is for the world to be saved. However, if we don't go out into the world, the world will remain lost. Two keys to remember are:

  Key #1: The world has not accepted the Truth God has revealed.
  Key #2: We have a responsibility to lead the world to the Truth.

Unit 1 Introduction

Unit Memory Verse

"The Lord is not slow in keeping His promise, as some understand slowness. He is patient with you, not wanting anyone to perish, but everyone to come to repentance." (2 Peter 3:9).

Unit 1 Introduction

God So Loved the World

Before the D-Team Experience

LEADER DEVOTION

Did you ever sing the children's song, "I am a Promise"? The song talks about the fact that we are all "promises" filled with possibility and potential. Are you living up to the claims of the song? In this lesson you will be challenging your students to understand what a promise is and what it means when God makes a promise. How are you doing as a promise-keeper? Do you realize that when you made a commitment to follow Christ, you also made a promise to spread the gospel every chance you're given? Are you doing this? Are you just talking about the possibilities for evangelism or are you acting on them? Are you just living with potential or are you turning your potential into results? Spend some time reflecting on how you have upheld your promise to God. Then spend some time in prayer. You might even feel the need to recommit your life to winning others for Christ.

LOOKING AHEAD

Student Focus
Every D-Team member will discover how much God loves the world by answering these three questions:
> Question #1: What is a promise?
> Question #2: What are some of God's promises?
> Question #3: What is the Ultimate Promise?

Unit Memory Verse
"The Lord is not slow in keeping His promise, as some understand slowness. He is patient with you, not wanting anyone to perish, but everyone to come to repentance" (2 Peter 3:9).

Practical Impact
During this D-Team experience, your students will write a "contract for life." In this contract, each student will have an opportunity to accept the promise God has made to us. The student will then make his or her own promise to God.

BE PREPARED

Materials Needed
- Bibles, notebooks, and pens
- Duplicated Student Notes
- Construction paper
- Felt-tip markers
- CD or tape player (Option 1)
- Business cards (Option 2)

Special Preparation
Prepare business cards with your name and phone number. Print your promise to your students on the card: *I will do my best to be there whenever you need me.* (Option 2)

Environment
To set up the environment for this D-Team experience, you can choose one of the following. Option 1 works in any setting; Option 2 moves the experience outside your normal setting.

Option 1: Contact a few students ahead of time and ask them to bring any CDs or tapes of songs that contain the words *promise, plan,* or *commitment.* Or have your students start the lesson by singing as many songs as they can think of that contain these words. Or bring in a video of a politician giving a speech filled with promises. Ask your students what they think it means to make a promise. You might even want to come up with a definition and display it in your room.

Option 2: Take your students to a "special spot" such as a park, forest, or pond. When you get to the spot, ask your students what it means to make a promise. After a brief discussion, tell your students that you are going to make a promise with them. Promise them that you will do your best to be there whenever they need you. Then give each student some sort of symbol to represent this promise. The symbol could be as simple as a business card with your telephone number. Tell them that whenever they look at this object, they should be reminded of the promise you have made.

Leading the D-Team Experience

(60 min. total)

GET STARTED

Unit Preview
Have a student read aloud the information under the "Unit Preview" in the Student Notes: *As you work together through "Unit 1: God's Plan for the World," you will discover God's plan by answering three questions:*
1. *What promise has God made to the world?*
2. *How should we respond to God's promise?*
3. *What is God's plan to reach the world?*

Unit Memory Verse
Read aloud 2 Peter 3:9, "The Lord is not slow in keeping His promise, as some understand slowness. He is patient with you, not wanting anyone to perish, but everyone to come to repentance." Explain that God is not indifferent to our sin; rather, He is a long-suffering God who is patiently waiting for everyone who will come to repentance.

Student Prayer
Have a student pray that your group members will listen and open their hearts to what God has to say.

Focus
Share with your group that during this D-Team experience, they will discover how much God loves the world by answering these three questions:

Question #1: What is a promise?
Question #2: What are some of God's promises?
Question #3: What is the Ultimate Promise?

THE EXPERIENCE

Question #1: What is a promise?
Ask your students: *List all the promises you have made with others or that others have made with you during the past year.* Have the students share their answers with a few people around them or share with the whole group.

Now ask them: *Write a definition for the word **promise**.* After a few of them share their definitions, display *Webster's* definition: "a declaration that one will do or refrain from doing something specified; reason to expect something; ground for expectation of success, improvement, or excellence."

Ask: *Does our society know how to keep promises? List examples of broken promises from society as well as your own personal experiences.*

Ask: *Have you ever known anybody who has never broken a promise?* (This includes being late, backing out of something, lying, etc.) Note that keeping a promise is a very difficult thing to accomplish because we are all human and therefore not perfect. Read aloud Romans 3:23 to your students. Explain that there is One person who has *never* broken a promise and who will *never* break a promise.

Question #2: What are some of God's promises?

Have each student (or pair of students if you have a large group) look up one of the following passages about a promise made by God. Tell them to read the passage and then be prepared to share a summary with the rest of the group.

Genesis 9:1–17—God promised Noah and his descendants that He would never again destroy man and the earth until His purposes for creation were fully realized.

Genesis 17:6–8—God promised Abraham that he would be blessed with land and more offspring than he could count.

Exodus 20:1–24—God gave Moses the promise of the Ten Commandments.

2 Samuel 7:1–17—God promised David that his dynasty would live forever.

After your students have shared the four examples of promises made by God, ask: *How do you know God kept these promises?* If time permits, have your students find verses which support their responses. Or assign your students some homework. Have them cite as many examples as possible where God upholds His promises. A hint for your students is that with one act God fulfilled a great promise. What was that one act?

Question #3: What is the Ultimate Promise?

Remind your students that so far we have answered two questions: "What is a promise?" and "What were some of God's promises?" Tell them that now that we know God will always hold true to a promise, it is important to focus on the one promise which has not yet been fulfilled—the Ultimate Promise.

Have a student **read aloud John 3:16.** Take a few moments to dissect this verse. Stress the importance of how each word in this verse works together to fulfill all of the past promises and all of the future promises.

Say: *John 3:16 tells us that whoever believes in Christ will be saved. What about those who never get a chance to hear?*

Explain that there is another promise God has made which has not yet been fulfilled. Have your students **read the following Scriptures: 1 Timothy 2:3–6 and 2 Peter 3:9.** Ask: *What do these verses have in common?* Give the students a few minutes to share their answers. They should realize that the Ultimate Promise which has not yet been fulfilled is that God won't return until everyone has heard the Truth! Ask: *What does this mean for us?*

 (5 min.)

REFLECTION

God has promised He won't return until everyone has heard about the way to eternal life. Tell your students that, for the next five to ten minutes, they are going to make a covenant with God. Today they learned about ways God made covenants with Noah, Abraham, Moses, and David. Now it is their turn to make a covenant. Ask your students to complete the Contract for Life in their Student Notes. Encourage them to take their contracts home and keep them in a place where they will be reminded of their covenant with God.

Give your students a few minutes to record honest responses to the following questions, found in their Student Notes: *What was most meaningful to you about our experience today? What does God want you to do in response?*

Ask a student to read aloud the Summary Statements in the Student Notes.

Prep Notes

Summary Statements

We learned today that . . .
- God loved the world He made and has kept His promises with humankind throughout the ages.
- We know what it means to make a promise.
- We know what some of God's original promises were.
- We know what God's ultimate promise is.
- It is now our turn to make a promise to spread the Gospel.

MAKE AN IMPACT

(10 min.)

. . . In Your Life
The Bible is filled with promises made by God and by Jesus. Challenge your students to spend some time looking for further examples of promises which were made and kept. Have your students write them down and bring them to next week's D-Team experience.

. . . With Accountability
Have the D-Team members form pairs to become accountability partners for the week and to work on the memory verse. Have each student write out the **Unit Memory Verse**.

Prayer
Bring the students back together and close the meeting with prayer.

1. God So Loved the World

Preview

As you work together through "Unit 1: God's Plan," you will discover God's plan by answering three questions:

1. What promise has God made to the world?
2. How should we respond to God's promise?
3. What is God's plan to reach the world?

Unit Memory Verse

"The Lord is not slow in keeping His promise, as some understand slowness. He is patient with you, not wanting anyone to perish, but everyone to come to repentance" (2 Peter 3:9).

Focus

This week you will discover how much God loves the world by answering these three questions.

THE EXPERIENCE

Question #1: What is a promise?

List all the promises you have made with others or that others have made with you during the past year.

Write a definition for the word *promise*.

MAKE AN IMPACT

. . . In Your Life

The Bible is filled with promises made by God and by Jesus. Spend some time looking for further examples of promises which were made and kept. Write them down and bring them to next week's group experience.

. . . With Accountability

With your accountability partner, talk about your responses to the "Reflection" questions. Exchange phone numbers. Call each other this week to hold each other accountable to making an impact in your lives.

name

phone

Begin learning your memory verse by writing it out in the space below.

MEMORY VERSE
2 Peter 3:9

Does our society know how to keep promises? List examples of broken promises from society as well as from your own personal experiences.

Have you ever known anybody who has never broken a promise?

Question #2: What are some of God's promises?
Read the following passages about a promise made by God.

Genesis 9:1-17

Genesis 17:6-8

Exodus 20:1-24

2 Samuel 7:1-17

How do you know God kept these promises?

Question #3: What is the Ultimate Promise?
Read John 3:16. John 3:16 tells us that whoever believes in Christ will be saved. What about those who never get a chance to hear?

Read 1 Timothy 2:3-6 and 2 Peter 3:9. What do these verses have in common?

REFLECTION

God has promised He won't return until everyone has heard about the way to eternal life. For the next five to ten minutes you are going to make a covenant with God. Today you learned about ways God made covenants with Noah, Abraham, Moses, and David. Now it is your turn to make a covenant.

Contract for Life

God has promised that He won't return until everyone has heard the Truth.

I, _____ , promise to
        (name)

_____

As a symbol of my commitment, I will

_____

_____

Signature _____   Date _____

What was most meaningful to you about our experience today?

What does God want you to do in response?

Summary Statements

We learned today that . . .
- God loved the world He made and has kept His promises with humankind throughout the ages.
- We know what it means to make a promise.
- We know what some of God's original promises were.
- We know what God's ultimate promise is.
- It is now our turn to make a promise to spread the Gospel.

Every Knee Shall Bow

2

Before the D-Team Experience

LEADER DEVOTION

"You show that you are a letter from Christ, the result of our ministry, written not with ink but with the Spirit of the living God, not on tablets of stone but on tablets of human hearts. Such confidence as this is ours through Christ before God. Not that we are competent in ourselves to claim anything for ourselves, but our competence comes from God. He has made us competent as ministers of a new covenant—not of the letter but of the Spirit; for the letter kills, but the Spirit gives life" (2 Cor. 3:3–6).

Reflect on this passage for a moment. What does it mean? What applications can be drawn for your life? What applications do you see for your ministry? What applications do you see for your students? After you spend some time in reflection and prayer, seek out someone with whom you will share your thoughts.

LOOKING AHEAD

Student Focus
Every D-Team member will discover two keys to understanding God's love for the world:
Key #1: Everyone is given the chance to hear God's Truth.
Key #2: Everyone has an opportunity to accept God's Truth.

Unit Memory Verse
"The Lord is not slow in keeping His promise, as some understand slowness. He is patient with you, not wanting anyone to perish, but everyone to come to repentance" (2 Peter 3:9).

Practical Impact
During this D-Team experience, your students will realize how important it is that the world doesn't just know that God exists, but that the world accepts God's awesome plan for salvation. During the Reflection, your students will participate in a time of commitment. They will bow before the Lord and the group and proclaim that He is Lord of their lives. They will also commit to going out into the world so that the world not only knows, but also accepts.

BE PREPARED

Materials Needed
- Bibles, notebooks, and pens
- Duplicated Student Notes

Special Preparation
Get permission from the proprietors of the supermarket, etc., to have your students do their survey. (Option 2)

Environment

To set up the environment for this D-Team experience, you can choose one of the following. Option 1 works in any setting; Option 2 moves the experience outside your normal setting.

Option 1: Have your students list all the people they can think of who have *never* heard of God or Jesus. After thinking for a few moments, your students will probably be hard-pressed to come up with a single name. Now tell your students that it does not have to be someone they know. Ask them if they think there is anyone in the world who has not heard of God or Jesus. This time you will probably get a few more answers, such as people living in third-world countries. Tell your students that the truth is that *everyone* in the world is given a chance to hear about God and His Son. The problem is that not everyone will accept. This is what today's experience is all about.

Option 2: Take your D-Team members on a "quest for truth." Plan to informally survey people outside a supermarket, shopping mall, bus or train station, or a restaurant. Have your students make up a list of questions they will ask such as: *Have you ever heard of God? Who is Jesus? How do you get to heaven?* The point of these questions is to find out if there is anyone in the world who has *not* heard of God and His Son, Jesus Christ. When you have finished, lead your students in a discussion about why the world knows the answers but simply refuses to bow down and accept.

Leading the D-Team Experience
(60 min. total)

GET STARTED
(5 min.) 🕐

Review
Have a student read aloud the information under "Review" in the Student Notes: *Last week's experience described this plan and promise made by God. This week we will learn that the world is given a chance to be saved, but they must accept it.*

Student Prayer
Have each student in your group pray for a different part of the world. Have them pray that every corner of the world will some day bow before their Lord and Maker.

Focus
Share with your group that during this D-Team experience, they will discover two keys to understanding God's love for the world:

Key #1: Everyone is given the chance to hear God's Truth.
Key #2: Everyone has an opportunity to accept God's Truth.

THE EXPERIENCE
(40 min.) 🕐

Key #1: Everyone is given the chance to hear God's Truth.
Remind your students that last week we talked about God's promise to the world. Explain that this experience deals with God's wrath, which will come to those who aren't willing to accept His promise.

Have a student *read aloud Romans 1:18–20.* Ask: *In verse 20, what does it mean "that men are without excuse"? Do you agree with this verse? What are some examples of ways God reveals Himself to the world? Have God's eternal power and divine nature ever been made clear to you? When or how?*

Note that God *does* reveal Himself to everyone in so many different ways. Now take some time to focus only on nature's role in revealing God. Ask your students: *List several ways God reveals Himself through nature.* (You might want to take your students outside if possible.) After they have listed the many awesome aspects of nature, comment that God's creation makes it impossible to think there is not a God.

Key #2: Everyone has an opportunity to accept God's Truth.
Ask your students: *If God's plan for the world is to reveal Himself to everyone, what is the next part of this plan?*

Have your students *read Romans 10:1–11.* Lead your students in a discussion using the following questions:

In verse 3, Paul talks about the fact that the Israelites did not know the righteousness that comes from God. Why didn't they? (Because they sought to establish their own.)

Prep Notes

What are some examples from our world where people might seek to establish their own righteousness? (Some examples might be trying to gain wealth or power or thinking that doing good deeds will get one into heaven.) **Do you think people attempt to establish their own righteousness because they have not heard the Truth, or because they don't want to accept the Truth?** (Students should respond that people have heard the Truth but they don't want to accept it.)

What is the end law that will bring righteousness to all who believe? What does this mean? (Christ is the end law. He came to fulfill God's promise by giving His life for our sins.)

What does verse 8 tell us about faith? (It tells us that faith is already in our hearts and in our mouths.)

In verses 9–11, God makes it known that in order to have eternal life, we must do what? (We must believe in our hearts and confess with our tongues that Jesus is Lord!) **Do you think this is an easy thing for people to do? Why or why not?**

Divide your students into pairs (or groups of three), and assign the following verses to each pair: *Isaiah 45:23–24; Philippians 2:10–11; Romans 14:11.* Tell them: **Read the verses and record the most important thing to remember about the passage.**

Have the students share their discoveries. What they should discover is that each of these verses tells us that we must bow before God and confess with our tongues if we truly want to be saved.

Now ask your students: **What do these passage mean for us? What do they mean for the world?** Emphasize that we must remember that just because we *know* what it takes to be saved does not mean we *are* saved. Many of us look for righteousness in all the wrong places. God's plan for the world is that everyone will hear His Truth. The world must accept this.

 (5 min.)

REFLECTION

Last week your students made a covenant with God. This week they will bow before God in front of the whole group. Dim the lights in your room and have the students form a circle holding hands. Read aloud Isaiah 45:22–25. Then have the students bow one at a time and repeat the phrase from verse 24: "In the Lord alone are righteousness and strength." Be aware of first timers who might not be ready to make this step. After you turn the lights back on, tell your students that they have heard and accepted, but the *real* task for us as Christians is to present the Truth to the world so others can bow and confess. If time permits, ask students when they first heard about God and when they accepted Jesus as their Savior and Lord.

Give your students a few minutes to record honest responses to the following questions, found in their Student Notes: **What was most meaningful to you about our experience today? What does God want you to do in response?**

Ask a student to read aloud the Summary Statements in the Student Notes.

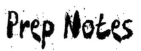

Summary Statements

We learned today that . . .
- God has made sure all humankind will be given the opportunity to hear the Truth before Jesus returns.
- The problem is that just because someone hears doesn't necessarily mean he or she understands or accepts the Truth.
- We know what needs to be done, so we must first believe and confess in our own lives and then venture out to share the Truth with our lost world.

MAKE AN IMPACT

(10 min.)

. . . In Your Life
Challenge your students to think of ways they can reach out to the world and share God's Truth. Tell your students to write out as many ways as they can think of to share the gospel. Tell them to be prepared to share their ideas at the next D-Team experience.

. . . With Accountability
Have the D-Team members form pairs to become accountability partners for the week and to work on the memory verse. Have each student write out the **Unit Memory Verse**.

Prayer
Bring the students back together and close with prayer.

2. Every Knee Shall Bow

Review

Last week's experience described this plan and promise made by God. This week we will learn that the world is given a chance to be saved, but they must accept it.

Focus

This week you will discover two keys to understanding God's love for the world.

Key #1: Everyone is given the chance to hear God's Truth.
Read Romans 1:18–20. In verse 20, what does it mean "that men are without excuse"?

Do you agree with this verse?

What are some examples of ways God reveals Himself to the world?

Have God's eternal power and divine nature ever been made clear to you? When or how?

List several ways God reveals Himself through nature.

Summary Statements

We learned today that . . .
- God has made sure that all humankind will be given the opportunity to hear the Truth before Jesus returns.
- The problem is that just because someone hears doesn't necessarily mean he or she understands or accepts the Truth.
- We know what needs to be done, so we must first believe and confess in our own lives and then venture out to share the Truth with our lost world.

MAKE AN IMPACT

. . . In Your Life
Try to think of ways you can reach out to the world and share God's Truth. Write out as many ways as you can think of to share the gospel. Be prepared to share your ideas at your next small group experience.

. . . With Accountability
With your accountability partner, talk about your responses to the "Reflection" questions. Exchange phone numbers. Call each other this week to hold each other accountable to making an impact in your lives.

name _____ phone _____

Review your memory verse by writing it out in the space below. Then recite it to your partner.

MEMORY VERSE
2 Peter 3:9

Key #2: Everyone has an opportunity to accept God's Truth.
If God's plan for the world is to reveal Himself to everyone, what is the next part of this plan?

Read Romans 10:1–11. In verse 3, Paul talks about the fact that the Israelites did not know the righteousness that comes from God. Why didn't they?

What are some examples from our world where people might seek to establish their own righteousness?

Do you think people attempt to establish their own righteousness because they have not heard the Truth, or because they don't want to accept the Truth?

What is the end law that will bring righteousness to all who believe? What does this mean?

What does verse 3 tell us about faith?

In verses 9–11, God makes it known that in order to have eternal life, we must do what? Do you think this is an easy thing for people to do? Why or why not?

Read the following passages and record the most important thing to remember about each passage.

Isaiah 45:23–24

Philippians 2:10–11

Romans 14:11

What do these passages mean for you? What do they mean for the world?

REFLECTION

Last week you made a covenant with God. This week you will bow before God in front of the whole group. Read Isaiah 45:22–25. Now bow and repeat the phrase from verse 24: "In the Lord alone are righteousness and strength."

What was most meaningful to you about our experience today?

What does God want you to do in response?

Impact the World

Before the D-Team Experience

LEADER DEVOTION

How is your Christian walk? As you prepare to speak to your students about the need to get out into the world, think about your role in the world. We are told to be in the world and not of the world, but this is not always an easy task. Read 2 Peter 1:3–10. Which of these qualities do you possess? Which of these qualities do you need to work on? Verse 9 tells us that if we don't possess these qualities we are blind or shortsighted. As we go through each day, we should be making an effort to obtain these qualities. As long as we practice these things (we are told in verse 10) we will never stumble. Commit to possessing these qualities daily.

LOOKING AHEAD

Student Focus
Every D-Team member will discover that God's plan is for the world to be saved. However, if we don't go out into the world, the world will remain lost. Two keys to remember are:

Key #1: The world has not accepted the Truth God has revealed.
Key #2: We have a responsibility to lead the world to the Truth.

Unit Memory Verse
"The Lord is not slow in keeping His promise, as some understand slowness. He is patient with you, not wanting anyone to perish, but everyone to come to repentance" (2 Peter 3:9).

Practical Impact
During this D-Team experience, your students will realize that the world has not accepted the Truth God has made known to them. Therefore, we must accept the responsibility of leading the world to the Truth. In the "Reflection" section your students will have the opportunity to select an area of the world for which they will be committed to pray. The group will partake in a circle of prayer and discuss a plan of action to reach the world.

BE PREPARED

Materials Needed
- Bibles, notebooks, and pens
- Duplicated Student Notes
- Map or Globe
- Thumbtacks or markers (to mark spots on the map)
- Newspaper and magazine articles (Option 1)
- Duplicated surveys (Option 2)

Special Preparation
- Clip newspaper and magazine articles that reflect worldly values such as power, wealth, beauty, etc. (Option 1).
- Prepare a simple survey with questions such as: *Have you ever heard of God? Do you believe He sent His Son, Jesus, to save you? Do you have a need to have a relationship with Jesus Christ? (Option 2).*

Environment
To set up the environment for this D-Team experience, you can choose one of the following. Option 1 works in any setting; Option 2 moves the experience outside your normal setting.

Option 1: Introduce this D-Team experience by demonstrating the depravity of the world. Last week you discussed the fact that everyone is given the chance to hear God's message. This week, help your students see the unfortunate condition of our world because there are so many who refuse to receive God's free gift. Bring in newspaper or magazine articles which demonstrate the world's values. Have an open discussion with your students about the world's values versus the values God wants us to uphold. We have all been given two paths to follow in life: One path leads to eternal damnation, the other leads to eternal life. Ask your students why a simple decision like this is so difficult to make.

Option 2: Take your D-Team members on another "quest for truth." Plan to survey people outside a supermarket, shopping mall, bus or train station, or a restaurant. Have your students administer the surveys you prepared ahead of time. When you have finished, lead your students in a discussion about the idea that even though everyone has heard of God, many don't feel a need to acknowledge that the only way to eternal life is through Jesus Christ.

Leading the D-Team Experience
(60 min. total)

GET STARTED

Review
Have a student read aloud the information under the "Review" in the Student Notes: *Last week we learned that the world is given a chance to be saved, but they must accept it. This week we'll examine an urgent message: If we don't impact the world, who will?*

Student Prayer
Have a student pray that the group will not be swayed by Satan's tempting or by the depravity of the world.

Focus
Share with your D-Team members that they will discover that God's plan is for the world to be saved. However, if they don't go out into the world, the world will remain lost. Two keys they can remember are:

Key #1: The world has not accepted the Truth God has revealed.
Key #2: We have a responsibility to lead the world to the Truth.

THE EXPERIENCE

Key #1: The world has not accepted the Truth God has revealed.
Remind your students that last week we talked about the fact that God has made Himself known to all humankind. However, just because God has made Himself known doesn't mean everyone accepts Him. This is where we come in. Part of the problem is that we are not just fighting against man, we are fighting against Satan.

Have a student *read aloud Romans 5:12.* Ask: *What does this verse indicate about sin?* (That ever since Adam and Eve committed original sin, we are all sinners.)

Select two students to read the following verses: *John 7:7 and 1 John 5:19.* Explain that these verses demonstrate that the world is controlled by evil. Now have your students read the parable of the weeds, found in Matthew 13:36–43. Discuss these questions: *In this parable, what does the good seed represent?* (the sons of the kingdom) *What does the field represent?* (the world) *What do the weeds represent?* (sons of the Evil One) *Who is the enemy who sows weeds?* (the devil) *What is the harvest?* (the end of the age) *What will happen at the end of the age?* (The weeds will be pulled up and thrown into the fire where they will spend eternity. The righteous will shine like the sun in God's kingdom.) *Do you think the world knows what will happen on judgment day? Do you think the world believes this will happen on judgment day?*

Key #2: We have a responsibility to lead the world to the Truth.
Ask: *Why do you think it is so difficult for the people in the world to acknowledge they are sinners and receive the free gift of eternal life God has offered?* Have your students list as many answers as possible. Emphasize that God has made known to us the path we should take. However, Satan has a tight grip on the world and is influencing many people not to accept God's gift. *Do you think it is*

Prep Notes

easier for the rich person in the world to receive this free gift or for the poor person? (Point out that it is equally difficult for a wealthy person and a poor person, for we all face temptations and struggles. They just come in different forms.)

So what can we do to lead the world to God's Truth? There are some people in this world whom we can try to convince until we are blue in the face, but it still seems useless. Two simple steps that we as Christians can take are: *(1) to lead with our lives and (2) lead with prayer.*

Lead with our lives
Read aloud the Parable of the sheep and the goats, found in Matthew 25:31–46. Have your students summarize the parable. Ask: *What does this parable mean in terms of your own life? What does it mean in terms of getting the world to accept Jesus as their Savior?* Give them a few minutes to respond and, if time permits, have the students share their answers in pairs or with the whole group.

Lead with prayer
Ask your students: *How many hours a week do you spend in prayer for the lost of this world? Write down how many hours a week you would like to spend praying for the lost of this world.*

Encourage your students: *Study the following verses on the power of prayer: Matthew 21:22; Romans 12:12; Colossians 4:2–4.*

🕐 **(5 min.)**

REFLECTION

The world is filled with organizations whose focus is to save the world. People are concerned with recycling, saving animals, saving trees, etc. As Christians, we should have an even stronger campaign because, after all, we are advocates for the most important thing of all—human souls.

Take out a map or globe and spend time just looking at it. Encourage your students to think of the billions of people who inhabit the earth who do not know Jesus as their Savior.

Summarize with your students that today we learned that when going out and preaching to the world seems futile, there are two other steps to be taken. The first one is to demonstrate to the world through our actions. The second is to pray. We will each mark off an area of the world which we will commit to pray for.

Spend the next ten minutes in a circle of prayer with each student praying for a specific area of the world. Students can pick anything from a continent to a city.

Give your students a few minutes to record honest responses to the following questions, found in their Student Notes: *What was most meaningful to you about our experience today? What does God want you to do in response?*

Ask a student to read aloud the Summary Statements in the Student Notes.

Summary Statements

We learned today that . . .
- God so loved the world He made and kept His promises with all humankind throughout the ages.
- God has made sure all humankind will be given the opportunity to hear the Truth before Jesus returns.
- We need to take responsibility and realize it us up to us to lead the world to God's Truth.
- Besides sharing the Truth with our mouths, we should be leading the world to the Truth through our actions as well as lifting up the world in prayer.

MAKE AN IMPACT

(10 min.)

. . . In Your Life
Challenge your students to commit to spending a specific amount of time in prayer for the lost of the world. Ask them to pray specifically for the area of the world they marked off on the map. They should also be praying for their own actions—that they will develop a willingness to help "the least of these."

. . . With Accountability
Have the D-Team members form pairs to become accountability partners for the week and to work on the memory verse. Have each student write out and recite the **Unit Memory Verse** to his or her partner. Then ask each pair to share the significance of the memory verse in his or her life.

Prayer
Bring the students back together and close with prayer.

3. Impact the World

Review

Last week we learned that the world is given a chance to be saved, but they must accept it. This week we'll examine an urgent message: If we don't impact the world, who will?

Focus

During this experience, you will discover that God's plan is for the world to be saved. However, if we don't go out into the world, the world will remain lost. We will be examining two keys to reaching a lost world.

THE EXPERIENCE

Key #1: The world has not accepted the Truth God has revealed.
Read Romans 5:12. What does this verse indicate about sin?

Read John 7:7 and 1 John 5:19. In this parable, what does the good seed represent?

What does the field represent?

What do the weeds represent?

Who is the enemy who sows weeds?

MAKE AN IMPACT

. . . In Your Life

Try to commit to spending a specific amount of time in prayer for the lost people of the world. Pray specifically for the area of the world you marked off on the map. You should also be praying for you own actions—that you will develop a willingness to help "the least of these."

. . . With Accountability

With your accountability partner, talk about your responses to the "Reflection" questions. Exchange phone numbers. Call each other this week to hold each other accountable to making an impact in your lives.

name	phone

Continue learning your memory verse by writing it in the space below and reciting it to your partner. Share with your partner the significance this memory verse has for your life.

MEMORY VERSE
2 Peter 3:9

What is the harvest?

What will happen at the end of the age?

Do you think the world knows what will happen on judgment day? Do you think the world believes this will happen on judgment day?

Key #2: We have a responsibility to lead the world to the Truth.
Why do you think it is so difficult for people in the world to acknowledge they are sinners and receive the free gift of eternal life God has offered?

Do you think it is easier for the rich person in the world to receive this free gift or easier for the poor person?

Lead with our lives
Read the parable of the sheep and the goats, found in Matthew 25:31–46. What does this parable mean in terms of your own life? What does it mean in terms of getting the world to accept Jesus as their Savior?

Lead with prayer
How many hours a week do you spend in prayer for the lost of this world?

Write down how many hours a week you would like to spend praying for the lost of this world.

Study the following verses on the power of prayer: Matthew 21:22; Romans 12:12; Colossians 4:2–4.

REFLECTION

Spend some time looking at the globe or map. Mark off an area of the world for which you will commit to pray.

Spend the next ten minutes in a circle of prayer, praying for a specific area of the world. You can pick anything from a continent to a city.

What was most meaningful to you about our experience today?

What does God want you to do in response?

Summary Statements

We learned today that . . .
- God so loved the world He made and kept His promises with all humankind throughout the ages.
- God has made sure all humankind will be given the opportunity to hear the Truth before Jesus returns.
- We need to take responsibility and realize it us up to us to lead the world to God's Truth.
- Besides sharing the Truth with our mouths, we should be leading the world to the Truth through our actions as well as lifting up the world in prayer.

LEADER FOCUS

Many Christians today have forgotten who they really are in Christ; they face an identity crisis. With this unit focusing on our identity as Christians, take a moment to ask yourself if the people around you know you as a believer. Would they say you are a "stranger in this land"? Take a few minutes to pray and ask God to soften your heart for what He wants to tell you.

BIG PICTURE

Unit Overview
In Unit 2 we will be focusing primarily on our identity as Christians as we live in this world by answering three questions: (1) Who am I? (2) How do I stay a stranger? (3) Why should I be a stranger in this world? Your students will walk away with a clearer perspective on their God-given identity in Christ.

1. Foreigners
During this D-Team experience, your students will answer the question, "Who am I?" by looking at two biblical truths:

> Truth #1: We are made in the image of God—our Creator.
> Truth #2: As Christians, we are strangers in this world.

2. Strangers
During this D-Team experience, your students will respond to the question, "How do I stay a stranger?" by discovering two answers:

> Answer #1: Don't conform to the patterns of this world.
> Answer #2: Be transformed by the renewing of your mind.

3. Ambassadors
Why should we be strangers in this world? Because it allows us the opportunity to be ambassadors to this foreign land. During this D-Team experience, your students will learn three facts that will help them understand their role as ambassadors for Jesus Christ:

> Fact #1: An ambassador is the highest-ranking personal representative of the person and dignity of the President.

STUDENT IMPACT

Fact #2: An ambassador has full responsibility to implement U.S. foreign policy in a country and is frequently entrusted with power.

Fact #3: An ambassador's personality and prestige play an important role in communicating the views of his or her government.

Unit Memory Verse
"We are therefore Christ's ambassadors, as though God were making His appeal through us. We implore you on Christ's behalf: Be reconciled to God" (2 Cor. 5:20).

Unit 2 Introduction

Foreigners

Before the D-Team Experience

LEADER DEVOTION

Take a few minutes to reflect on what A. W. Tozer once said regarding the relationship between God and man: "Every soul belongs to God and exists by his pleasure. God being who and what he is, and we being who and what we are, the only thinkable relation between us is one of full lordship on his part and complete submission on ours. We owe him every honor that it is in our power to give Him" (*Draper's Quotations for the Christian World,* Tyndale, 242).

Pour out your praise and worship to God before you proceed with your preparation. May you be refreshed by His presence. As you prepare to lead, jot down your personal experiences and insights in the "Prep Notes" column so you can share them with your students.

LOOKING AHEAD

Student Focus
During this D-Team experience, your students will answer the question, "Who am I?" by looking at two biblical truths:
    Truth #1: We are made in the image of God—our Creator.
    Truth #2: As Christians, we are strangers in this world.

Unit Memory Verse
"We are therefore Christ's ambassadors, as though God were making His appeal through us. We implore you on Christ's behalf: Be reconciled to God" (2 Cor. 5:20).

Practical Impact
Your students will be taking a look at the identity they have been given as Christians in this world. They will be receiving mirrors to take home and remind them they are created to be a reflection of God's character.

BE PREPARED

Materials Needed
  • Bibles, notebooks, and pens
  • Duplicated Student Notes
  • Map and resources of the country you have chosen to study
  • Mirrors—small handheld or wallet size (You could write the verse Genesis 1:27 on it with a paint marker.)

Special Preparation
  • Choose a foreign country that is very different than your own. Do a little research at your local library and record different cultural aspects or characteristics about that country that make it unique. Duplicate some articles or pictures. Make enough for each of your students to have at least one article to study. You may

want to look at such cultural differences as food, clothing, different laws, rules, government structure, etc.
- If you can't find artifacts from the country you have chosen to study, try to provide some pictorial dictionaries or magazines with pictures of cultural objects. (Option 1)

Environment
To set up the environment for this D-Team experience, you can choose one of the following. Option 1 works in any setting; Option 2 moves the experience outside your normal setting.

Option 1: During this D-Team experience, you will be taking a look at a foreign country and all the aspects that make it different from your own culture. After selecting that country, get a map and some artifacts that would give a sense of what makes it different from your own culture. Display these artifacts around your meeting room.

Option 2: Take your students to a restaurant that serves the type of food found in your chosen country. Or arrange to meet at a location that would make your students feel like strangers. (For example: a college cafe, elderly home, corporate building, etc.) Get permission ahead of time!

Leading the D-Team Experience
(60 min. total)

GET STARTED

Unit Preview
Have a student read aloud the information under the "Preview" in the Student Notes:
As you work together through "Unit 2: Identity Crisis," you will be focusing primarily on your identity as a Christian as you live in this world by answering three questions:
1. *Who am I?*
2. *How do I stay a stranger?*
3. *Why should I be a stranger in this world?*

Unit Memory Verse
Read aloud 2 Corinthians 5:20, "We are therefore Christ's ambassadors, as though God were making His appeal through us. We implore you on Christ's behalf: Be reconciled to God." Explain that God has been reestablishing our relationship with Him ever since sin broke that relationship. In one sense, reconciliation is already done; in another sense, it's necessary to tell people about it.

Student Prayer
Ask a student to pray that God would show each student a fresh perspective on his or her identity.

Focus
Share with your students that during this D-Team experience, they will answer the question, "Who am I?" by looking at two biblical truths:

Truth #1: We are made in the image of God—our Creator.
Truth #2: As Christians, we are strangers in this world.

THE EXPERIENCE

Open this D-Team experience by explaining that you will be taking an imaginary trip to visit the country you chose. In order to be prepared, your students will need to start familiarizing themselves with the country and its customs. Now ask your students to take ten minutes to study the country you have chosen. Ask each student to come up with two ways that the customs and lifestyles of the people from the chosen country would be different from their own. Ask your students how they would be strangers in that land. Take a few minutes to hear their answers. Explain that we *are* strangers in a strange land, but we don't have to feel as if we are strangers to God.

Truth #1: We are made in the image of God—our Creator.
Read aloud Genesis 1:27. Ask: ***What can we learn about our creation from this verse?*** (We were created in the image of God. There is something of His very essence in each of us. He made us that way.) Emphasize that we have the potential to mirror God's character just as a face is reflected in a pool of water.

Read aloud Genesis 3:8–9. Ask: ***What do these verses indicate about God's desire for a relationship with humans?*** (Point out that these two verses show us God's desire to have fellowship with us. He created humans to have an intimate relationship with Him.) ***What broke that relationship?*** (Unfortunately, sin broke the uninhibited relationship Adam and Eve had with their Creator.) ***What was God's plan to renew that relationship with humans?*** (That intimate relationship was so important to God, He designed a plan of reconciliation. Jesus Christ offers a way for us to reconcile and renew that relationship.)

Truth #2: As Christians, we are strangers in this world.
Have a student ***read aloud 1 Peter 1:1 and 2:11.*** Pose this question: ***To whom do you think Peter was referring when he said, "To God's elect, strangers in the world"?*** (He was addressing the Christians.) ***Why are Christians referred to as strangers?*** (We are only temporarily residing on earth because our home is in heaven.)

Explain that God does not command us to be strangers. If we are Christians, then we have reestablished that intimate relationship with our Creator through Jesus Christ. Until we are at home in heaven with our Maker, we will live in a place that does not revolve around worshiping God. God has allowed Satan to rule over those who follow him.

Read aloud Ephesians 2:1–2. Ask: ***What do these verses indicate about Satan's power?*** (Satan has been given the freedom to roam the earth doing what he pleases to deceive people. Therefore this world is not our home: we are strangers. Our true home is the eternal place that God is creating for us—heaven!)

In summary, who are we? We are made in the image of God, and we are strangers on this earth. At the next D-Team experience, we will learn more about how to *stay* strangers in this crazy world.

(5 min.)

REFLECTION

Today, we learned about God's given identity to His children. We are made in the image of God and, therefore, we are strangers in this world. Ask your students to take a moment to evaluate their lives by deciding whether the following two statements are true for them: (1) I am made in the image of God and (2) I am a stranger in this world. Ask them if there is any area in their life that doesn't reflect either of these statements? Is so, what is it?

Give your students a few minutes to record honest responses to the following questions, found in their Student Notes: ***What was most meaningful to you about our experience today? What does God want you to do in response?***

Ask a student to read aloud the Summary Statements in the Student Notes.

Summary Statements

We learned today that . . .
- God designed us to have an intimate relationship with Him.
- God created us in His image to mirror His character.
- If we become one of His children, we are strangers in the world in which we live.

MAKE AN IMPACT

. . . In Your Life

We are not asked by our Creator to be strangers alone and on our own. He longs to walk and talk with us daily. After all, He created us to be intimate with Him! The area you wrote down in the "Reflection" section doesn't have to be conquered alone—you need to allow God to help you.

Challenge your students to commit to spending five minutes a day praying to their Heavenly Father regarding this issue, and anything else that is weighing heavily on them. Remind your students that God has provided them with a companion, the Holy Spirit.

If your students make this commitment to pray, then challenge them to sign their name in the space indicated in their Student Notes as a personal agreement between them and God. As they sign their Student Notes, give them mirrors to take home as a reminder that they are a reflection of God.

. . . With Accountability

Have the D-Team members form pairs to become accountability partners for the week and to work on the memory verse. Have each student write out the **Unit Memory Verse**.

Prayer

Bring the students back together and close with prayer.

1. Foreigners

Preview

As you work together through "Unit 2, Identity Crisis," you will be focusing primarily on your identity as a Christian as you live in this world by answering three questions:

1. Who am I?
2. How do I stay a stranger?
3. Why should I be a stranger in this world?

Unit Memory Verse

"We are therefore Christ's ambassadors, as though God were making His appeal through us. We implore you on Christ's behalf: Be reconciled to God" (2 Cor. 5:20).

Focus

Today you will answer the question, "Who am I?" looking at two biblical truths.

THE EXPERIENCE

Truth #1: We are made in the image of God—our Creator.
Read Genesis 1:27. What can we learn about our creation from this verse?

Read Genesis 3:8–9. What do these verses indicate about God's desire for a relationship with humans?

What broke that relationship?

"Reflection" questions. Exchange phone numbers. Call each other this week to hold each other accountable to making an impact in your lives.

name	phone

Begin learning your memory verse by writing it out in the space below.

MEMORY VERSE
2 Corinthians 5:20

What was God's plan to renew that relationship with humans?

Why are Christians referred to as strangers?

Truth #2: As Christians, we are strangers in this world.
Read 1 Peter 1:1 and 2:11. To whom do you think Peter was referring when he said, "To God's elect, strangers in the world"?

Read Ephesians 2:1–2. What do these verses indicate about Satan's power?

R E F L E C T I O N

Today you learned about God's given identity to His children. We are made in the image of God and, therefore, we are strangers in this world. Take a moment to evaluate your life. Are the following statements true for you?

I am made in the image of God.
I am a stranger in this world.

Is there any area in your life that doesn't reflect either of these statements? If so, what is it?

What was most meaningful to you about our experience today?

What does God want you to do in response?

Summary Statements

We learned today that . . .
- God designed us to have an intimate relationship with Him.
- God created us in His image to mirror His character.
- If we become one of His children, we are strangers in the world in which we live.

M A K E A N I M P A C T

. . . In Your Life
Try to commit to spending five minutes a day praying to your Heavenly Father regarding the issue you recorded in the "Reflection" section and anything else that is weighing heavily on you. Remember, God has provided you with a companion, the Holy Spirit.

If you make this commitment to pray, then sign your name below as a personal agreement between you and God. As you sign your name, you will be given a mirror to take home as a reminder that you are a reflection of God.

Signature:

. . . With Accountability
With your accountability partner, talk about your responses to the

Strangers

Before the D-Team Experience

LEADER DEVOTION

Paul writes in his letter to the Corinthians, "For we are the temple of the living God. As God has said: 'I will live with them and walk among them, and I will be their God, and they will be My people. Therefore come out from them and be separate,' says the Lord" (2 Cor. 6:16b–17a). What was Paul saying to us in this passage? He wants us to keep a distinction between us and the world. There should be a noticeable difference between the two. The easiest way to go about this is to continually seek God's face. If you are going in that direction, you won't have time to notice the world and its enticements. As you prepare to lead, jot down your personal experiences and insights in the "Prep Notes" column so you can share them with your students.

LOOKING AHEAD

Student Focus
During this D-Team experience, your students will respond to the question, "How do I stay a stranger?" by discovering two answers:
Answer #1: Don't conform to the patterns of this world.
Answer #2: Be transformed by the renewing of your mind.

Unit Memory Verse
"We are therefore Christ's ambassadors, as though God were making His appeal through us. We implore you on Christ's behalf: Be reconciled to God" (2 Cor. 5:20).

Practical Impact
Your students will be comparing being strangers in a foreign country to being strangers as Christians in this world.

BE PREPARED

Materials Needed
- Bibles, notebooks, and pens
- Duplicated Student Notes
- Research material regarding the country you studied at the last D-Team experience
- Chalkboard or flip chart

Environment

To set up the environment for this D-Team experience, you can choose one of the following. Option 1 works in any setting; Option 2 moves the experience outside your normal setting.

Option 1: Continue to display all the data on the country you selected for your hypothetical visit during your last D-Team experience.

Option 2: Try meeting in an area such as a large mall that will allow your students to see a diversity of people walking around.

Leading the D-Team Experience
(60 min. total)

GET STARTED

Review
Have a student read aloud the information under the "Review" in the Student Notes: *Last week, you were challenged to commit to spending five minutes a day praying about the issue you wrote down in the "Reflection" section. Were you able to fulfill that commitment?*

Student Prayer
Ask a student to pray that God will help each D-Team member understand how to be a stranger in this world.

Focus
Share with your D-Team members that this week they will respond to the question, "How do I stay a stranger?" by discovering two answers:

Answer #1: Don't conform to the patterns of this world.
Answer #2: Be transformed by the renewing of your mind.

THE EXPERIENCE

Begin this D-Team experience by suggesting that your students imagine they have been asked to live in a foreign country (the country you studied in D-Team #4) for one year.

Say: *Imagine you are a foreign exchange student for a school year. But you must come back home the same way you left. You must stay as culturally true to your hometown community as the day you left. How will you do that?*

Ask each student to come up with two methods he or she thinks will work. Invite each student to share ideas. Make a list on a flip chart or the chalkboard and discuss the ideas for a few minutes. Explain that this isn't a time to criticize other ideas, but to brainstorm how to better the ideas.

Answer #1: Don't conform to the patterns of this world.
Ask your students to open their Bibles to **Romans 12:2** and have one student read the verse aloud. Share with your students that the word *conform* means "together with or accompanied; associated with a figure or shape." Tell them that in Romans 12:2, Paul is referring to conformity to the world. In other words, we should not be together with or associated with or accompanied by this world any longer. When Paul talks about the world, he is saying we should cut ourselves off from what the world has to offer, not from non-Christians. All people matter to God, and they should matter to us too.

To find out what Paul meant, take the next few minutes to dig into the verse. Ask: *What did Paul mean by conforming to the patterns of the world? Did Paul mean that we can't party any more—no smoking, drinking, swearing, etc.? Were these the patterns he was talking about?* Note that Paul was referring to more than just avoiding the world's entertainment offers that take us down the path of sin. He was also referring to how we use our time and spend our money.

Remind your students that this world is on a one-way track that is self-centered. Satan encourages any action that will bring self-satisfaction. As believers, who are we desiring to please? We desire to please God. If the world is self satisfying, then it has nothing to offer that will be pleasing to God. Our refusal to conform to this world's values, however, has to go deeper than our actions. It's possible for us to avoid most of the customs of this world but still be proud, selfish, stubborn, and arrogant. Renewal must start in our minds and hearts.

Answer #2: Be transformed by the renewing of your mind.
Have a student *read aloud Romans 8:5–9.* Ask: *How can we be transformed rather than conformed? How would you describe the difference between focusing on what God wants you to do today that will bring glory to Him rather than focusing on what you can't do anymore now that you are a Christian?*

Point out that we are transformed by the renewing of our minds. The Holy Spirit can renew, reteach, and change the direction of our hearts and minds. We are not to allow the world to dictate our actions. God commands us to renew our minds by allowing His Holy Spirit to infiltrate our minds so that the choices we make and the actions we take will bring glory and honor to God—not ourselves.

Say: *Reflect back on your list of methods to stay a stranger in a foreign country. Will any of your earlier ideas help you stay focused on what you learned today? Will you be able to use any of the ideas proposed to help you stay a stranger in this world?*

 (5 min.)

REFLECTION

Your students have taken the time to study a Scripture that helps them define what being strangers in this world may mean for them. The next step for your students is to apply the lesson learned today. Ask your students to review a typical week in their life. As your students evaluate their lives and the day-to-day, week-to-week routines they go through, ask them the following questions: *Which of your choices have been or are influenced by the world? Which ones are made with a renewed mind? Which ones need to be changed? Why? How?*

Help your students come up with some solid answers. Encourage them to be honest with themselves, because their honesty will allow them to clearly assess where changes need to be made.

Give your students a few minutes to record honest responses to the following questions, found in their Student Notes: *What was most meaningful to you about our experience today? What does God want you to do in response?*

Ask a student to read aloud the Summary Statements in the Student Notes.

Summary Statements

We learned today that . . .
- As children of God, we should not be conformed to this world.
- Renewing our minds will help us stay focused on what God can do in our lives.
- Our day-to-day choices need to be made with daily renewed minds.

MAKE AN IMPACT

. . . In Your Life
Ask your students how they will begin to renew their minds during this next week. What is one area in which they can choose to be different this next week? Will their choice affect anyone else around them? Who and how? Will others be able to notice a difference in them? Ask your students to record their responses and be prepared to share their answer to the last question.

. . . With Accountability
Have the D-Team members form pairs to become accountability partners for the week and to work on the memory verse. Have each student write out the **Unit Memory Verse**.

Prayer
Bring the students back together and close with prayer.

5. Strangers

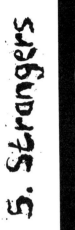

Review

Last week, you were challenged to commit to spending five minutes a day praying about the issue you wrote down in the "Reflection" section. Were you able to fulfill that commitment?

Focus

During this experience, you will respond to the question, "How do I stay a stranger?" by discovering two answers.

THE EXPERIENCE

Imagine you are a foreign exchange student for a school year. But you must come back home the same way you left. You must stay as culturally true to your hometown community as the day you left. How will you do that?

Come up with two methods you think will work.

Answer #1: Don't conform to the patterns of this world.
Read Romans 12:2. What did Paul mean by conforming to the patterns of the world? Did Paul mean that we can't party any more—no smoking, drinking, swearing, etc.? Were these the patterns he was talking about?

. . . With Accountability
With your accountability partner, talk about your responses to the "Reflection" questions. Exchange phone numbers. Call each other this week to hold each other accountable to making an impact in your lives.

name _____ phone _____

Continue learning your memory verse by writing it in the space below and reciting it to your partner.

MEMORY VERSE
2 Corinthians 5:20

Answer #2: Be transformed by the renewing of your mind.
Read Romans 8:5–9. How can we be transformed rather than conformed?

How would you describe the difference between focusing on what God wants you to do today that will bring glory to Him, rather than focusing on what you can't do anymore now that you are a Christian?

Reflect back on your list of methods to stay a stranger in a foreign country. Will any of your earlier ideas help you stay focused on what you learned today? Will you be able to use any of the ideas proposed to help you stay a stranger in this world?

REFLECTION

Review a typical week in your life. As you evaluate your life and the day-to-day, week-to-week routine you go through, consider the following questions:

Which of your choices have been or are influenced by the world?

Which ones are made with a renewed mind?

Which ones need to be changed? Why? How?

What was most meaningful to you about our experience today?

What does God want you to do in response?

Summary Statements

We learned today that . . .

- As children of God, we should not be conformed to this world.
- Renewing our minds will help us stay focused on what God can do in our lives.
- Our day-to-day choices need to be made with daily renewed minds.

MAKE AN IMPACT

. . . In Your Life
During this next week, how will you begin to renew your mind?

What is one area in which you can choose to be different this next week?

Will your choice affect anyone else around you? Who and how?

Will others be able to notice a difference in you next week?

Ambassadors

Before the D-Team Experience

LEADER DEVOTION

To prepare for this D-Team experience, open your Bible to Matthew 28:18–20. Read these verses aloud to yourself. These are Christ' words to us before He ascended into heaven. Are you fulfilling the Great Commission? Don't assume that just because you are leading this D-Team experience you are fulfilling God's commission to you. Take a moment and let the Holy Spirit speak to your heart. What is He saying to you? As you prepare to lead, jot down your personal experiences and insights in the "Prep Notes" column so you can share them with your students.

LOOKING AHEAD

Student Focus
Why should we be strangers in this world? Because it allows us the opportunity to be ambassadors to this foreign land. During this D-Team experience, your students will learn three facts that will help them understand their role as ambassadors for Jesus Christ:

Fact #1: An ambassador is the highest-ranking personal representative of the person and dignity of the President.

Fact #2: An ambassador has full responsibility to implement U.S. foreign policy in a country and is frequently entrusted with power.

Fact #3: An ambassador's personality and prestige play an important role in communicating the views of his or her government.

Unit Memory Verse
"We are therefore Christ's ambassadors, as though God were making His appeal through us. We implore you on Christ's behalf: Be reconciled to God" (2 Cor. 5:20).

Practical Impact
Your students will be looking at what an American ambassador is, and relating it to the call we have as believers to be Ambassadors for Jesus Christ.

BE PREPARED

Materials Needed
- Bibles, notebooks, and pens
- Duplicated Student Notes
- Photos and articles about ambassadors
- Military props (Option 1)
- Ambassador chart

Special Preparation

- Prepare for this D-Team experience by studying whatever information you can find at your local library on ambassadors. Bring photos and articles through which your students can browse.
- Make a large chart with the following heading: *Jesus Christ's Diplomatic Offices—Foreign Service.* Under the heading, create two columns. In the left column, titled *Country/Embassy Ambassador,* make a list of towns and schools near your church. Leave the right column blank for your students to sign their names.

Environment

To set up the environment for this D-Team experience, you can choose one of the following. Option 1 works in any setting; Option 2 moves the experience outside your normal setting.

Option 1: Arrange your room to look like a formal office in an embassy. Your students will be able to get into the whole idea of being an ambassador with some added props, such as an American flag and flags or banners from other countries.

Option 2: Have your D-Team members meet on a hill that overlooks the community where your students live. Another option would be to meet in a parking lot at your local high school.

Leading the D-Team Experience
(60 min. total)

GET STARTED

Review
Have a student read aloud the information under the "Review" in the Student Notes: *Last week, you began to determine how to renew your mind. You were asked about one area in which you could choose to be different and whether that choice would affect anyone else around you. Do you think others will notice a difference in you this week?*

Student Prayer
Ask a student to pray that God will teach each D-Team member how to be an ambassador for Christ.

Focus
Share with your students that today they will learn three facts that will help them understand their role as ambassadors for Jesus Christ:

Fact #1: **An ambassador is the highest-ranking personal representative of the person and dignity of the President.**
Fact #2: **An ambassador has full responsibility to implement U.S. foreign policy in a country and is frequently entrusted with power.**
Fact #3: **An ambassador's personality and prestige play an important role in communicating the views of his or her government.**

THE EXPERIENCE

(40 min.)

Begin this D-Team experience by asking: *Do you know what an ambassador is? What are the responsibilities of an ambassador?* Explain that an ambassador is the highest rank of diplomatic representative sent by one government to another. Tell your students that an ambassador's responsibilities include negotiating agreements between the U.S. and the host country, explaining and disseminating official U.S. policy, and maintaining cordial relations with that country's government and people. Ambassadors have full responsibility for implementing U.S. foreign policy by any and all U.S. government personnel (except those under military commands) within their country of assignment.

Explain to your students that there are three facts about ambassadors that can add depth to what Paul's message is regarding our role as ambassadors for Christ.

Fact #1: An ambassador is the highest ranking personal representative of the person and dignity of the President.
Ask a student to *read aloud 2 Corinthians 5:20 and John 15:16.* Ask: *What are some of the distinctive characteristics of an ambassador?* Emphasize that an ambassador is *chosen.* Your students have been chosen also to do the work of Christ and bear fruit.

Point out that an ambassador has the enormous responsibility of being an honest representative. Have a student *read aloud Acts 1:8.* Ask: *Based on this verse, in what ways are we to be ambassadors of Christ? What was the last challenge*

Jesus left with His disciples before being taken up into heaven?

Fact #2: An ambassador has full responsibility to implement U.S. foreign policy in a country and is frequently entrusted with power.
Explain to your students that there are certain "policies" ambassadors of Christ are to implement. Paul touches on several of them in ***Ephesians 4:22–5.21.*** Have your students quickly read the passage. Then ask: **List some "policies" ambassadors are called to implement.** Note that we are called to be ambassadors not only to nonbelievers, but to believers as well.

Remind your students that in Acts 1:8 we are told we will receive power to be an ambassador through the Holy Spirit who lives in each believer.

Fact #3: An ambassador's personality and prestige play an important role in communicating the views of his or her government.
Have your students ***read 1 Corinthians 10:31–11:1.*** Remind them that we don't have to offend people to get their attention. We can influence their choices by being different and setting an example in all that we do. We must always be aware that someone may be investigating who Jesus is and observing us without our knowing, and that each of our actions is speaking volumes to those around us. We must ask ourselves, "Will this choice point people toward or away from Christ?"

Summarize that there are three primary characteristics of an ambassador for Christ: first, we are chosen and asked to be Jesus' witnesses or representatives to the world; second, we are given power to implement and live by certain guidelines and policies; and third, an ambassador has the ability to influence people's choices about Christ by setting an example to live by.

 (5 min.)

REFLECTION

The next step for your students would be for them to take the information they learned today and determine if they would like to be an active ambassador for Christ. Display the chart that you prepared ahead of time and explain to your students that there are "foreign" mission fields right in their backyards. Explain that being an ambassador doesn't mean we have to leave the country. We are ambassadors to *all* who don't know Jesus personally. Invite your students to put their name in a space next to a "country" where they would like to serve as ambassador.

Give them a few minutes to quietly walk up and sign the chart. Explain to your students that just because they signed up for one area doesn't mean they aren't ambassadors anywhere else.

Give your students a few minutes to record honest responses to the following questions, found in their Student Notes: **What was most meaningful to you about our experience today? What does God want you to do in response?**

Ask a student to read aloud the Summary Statements in the Student Notes.

Summary Statements

We learned today that . . .
- We are chosen to be ambassadors for Christ.
- We have received power to be ambassadors.
- We are responsible to be witnesses for Christ.
- Our actions could influence someone's decision to follow Christ.

MAKE AN IMPACT

. . . In Your Life
Challenge each student to tell two people about his or her decision to become an ambassador for Christ. Then ask your students to consider what they could change about their life that would aid in their pursuit of being an ambassador?"

. . . With Accountability
Have the D-Team members form pairs to become accountability partners for the week and to work on the memory verse. Have each student write out and recite the **Unit Memory Verse** to his or her partner. Then ask each pair to share the significance of the memory verse in his or her life.

Prayer
Bring your students back together and close with prayer.

3. Ambassadors

Review

Last week, you began to determine how to renew your mind. You were asked about one area in which you could choose to be different and whether that choice would affect anyone else around you. Do you think others will notice a difference in you this week?

Focus

Why should we be strangers in this world? Because it allows us the opportunity to be ambassadors to this foreign land. This week, you will learn three facts that will help you understand your role as an ambassador for Jesus Christ.

THE EXPERIENCE

Do you know what an ambassador is?

What are the responsibilities of an ambassador?

Fact #1: An ambassador is the highest-ranking personal representative of the person and dignity of the President.
Read 2 Corinthians 5:20 and John 15:16. What are some of the distinctive characteristics of an ambassador?

. . . With Accountability
With your accountability partner, talk about your responses to the "Reflection" questions. Exchange phone numbers. Call each other this week to hold each other accountable to making an impact in your lives.

name _____

phone _____

Continue learning your memory verse by writing it in the space below and reciting it to your partner. Share with your partner the significance this memory verse has for your life.

MEMORY VERSE
2 Corinthians 5:20

Read Acts 1:8. Based on this verse, in what ways are we to be ambassadors of Christ?

What was the last challenge Jesus left with His disciples before being taken up into heaven?

Fact #2: An ambassador has full responsibility to implement U.S. foreign policy in a country and is frequently entrusted with power.
Read Ephesians 4:29–5:21. List some "policies" ambassadors of Christ are to implement.

Fact #3: An ambassador's personality and prestige play an important role in communicating the views of his or her government.
Read 1 Corinthians 10:31–11:1. Record your observations.

REFLECTION

After viewing the chart that explains that there are "foreign" mission fields right in your backyard, consider putting your name in a space next to a "country" where you would like to serve as ambassador.

Note that just because you signed up for one area doesn't mean you aren't an ambassador anywhere else.

What was most meaningful to you about our experience today?

What does God want you to do in response?

Summary Statements

We learned today that . . . .
- We are chosen to be ambassadors for Christ.
- We have received power to be ambassadors.
- We are responsible to be witnesses for Christ.
- Our actions could influence someone's decision to follow Christ.

MAKE AN IMPACT

. . . In Your Life
Commit to telling two people about your decision to become an ambassador for Christ. Who will those two people be?

What could you change about your life that would aid in your pursuit of being an ambassador?

LEADER FOCUS

Think for a moment about a missionary you know. Spend the next few moments in prayer for this person. You might even want to contact this person by phone or through a support letter. Let the person know you are praying for him or her and are willing to help in any way you can.

BIG PICTURE

Unit Overview
In Unit 3 we will be focusing on missions by answering three questions: (1) What are missions? (2) Why are missions important? (3) How can we support missions?

1. Global Messengers
During this D-Team experience, your students will discover that missions are a vital part of Christianity by answering three questions:

Question #1: What is a missionary?
Question #2: Why do we have missionaries?
Question #3: What do missionaries do?

2. A Visit from Afar
During this D-Team experience, your students will learn why missions are important through two firsthand encounters:

Encounter #1: Meet a missionary.
Encounter #2: Support a missionary.

3. Armchair Missionaries
During this D-Team experience, your students will learn how to be armchair missionaries by taking three steps:

Step #1: Support missionaries through letters.
Step #2: Support missionaries through offerings.
Step #3: Support missionaries through prayers.

Unit Memory Verse
"For we do not preach ourselves, but Jesus Christ as Lord, and ourselves as your servants for Jesus' sake" (2 Cor. 4:5).

Global Messengers

Before the D-Team Experience

LEADER DEVOTION

As you prepare to start this unit on missionaries, reflect for a moment about the role missions has played in your life. Your students will probably have many questions about this topic, so be sure to think through the following questions before you begin the lesson: *Do you support a missionary? Would you consider yourself a missionary? Have you ever been on a missions trip? Do you have to leave the country to be a missionary? Is there a need for missionaries in the U.S.? How old do you have to be to be a missionary? Are missionaries called by God? How do you know if you should be a missionary? How do missionaries know where to go?*

There are not necessarily right or wrong answers to these questions. However, it would benefit both you and your students if you spent time reflecting, looking up verses, and praying about these issues. As you prepare to lead, jot down your personal experiences and insights in the "Prep Notes" column so you can share them with your students.

LOOKING AHEAD

Student Focus
During this D-Team experience, your students will discover that missions are a vital part of Christianity by answering three questions:
   Question #1: What is a missionary?
   Question #2: Why do we have missionaries?
   Question #3: What do missionaries do?

Unit Memory Verse
"For we do not preach ourselves, but Jesus Christ as Lord, and ourselves as your servants for Jesus' sake" (2 Cor. 4:5).

Practical Impact
During this experience, each student will learn the who, why, and how of missionary work. They will end this experience by writing an imaginary letter in which they identify their own gifts. In this letter, each student must decide where he or she would like to be stationed as well as what type of work he or she might like to do.

BE PREPARED

Materials Needed
- Bibles, notebooks, and pens
- Duplicated Student Notes
- Stationery for each student

Special Preparation

Environment

To set up the environment for this D-Team experience, you can choose one of the following. Option 1 works in any setting; Option 2 moves the experience outside your normal setting.

Option 1: Begin this experience by painting a powerful picture of the need for missionaries in our world. Bring in a clip from a movie such as *The Mission*. Or bring in a scrapbook, photo album, or journal from any mission trips you might have taken. You could also read excerpts from books or journals written by missionaries. The stories of Samuel Morris, William Carey, and Jim Elliot are among the many powerful accounts to choose from.

Option 2: Take your D-Team members to a church library or Christian bookstore to gather information on missionaries. Your students may want to select a book about missionaries that interests them. Another idea would be to have a contest to see how many books you can find about missionaries serving in different countries of the world.

Leading the D-Team Experience
(60 min. total)

GET STARTED	*(5 min.)*

Unit Preview
Have a student read aloud the information under "Preview" in the Student Notes: *As you work together through "Unit 3: Mission: Possible," you will be focusing on missions by answering three questions:*
   1. *What are missions?*
   2. *Why are missions important?*
   3. *How can we support missions?*

Unit Memory Verse
Read aloud 2 Corinthians 4:5, "For we do not preach ourselves, but Jesus Christ as Lord, and ourselves as your servants for Jesus' sake," emphasizing that true followers of Christ are not puffed up with self-importance.

Student Prayer
Have a student pray for the missionaries of the world.

Focus
Share with your D-Team members that during this D-Team experience they will discover that missions are a vital part of Christianity by answering three questions:

Question #1: What is a missionary?
Question #2: Why do we have missionaries?
Question #3: What do missionaries do?

THE EXPERIENCE	*(40 min.)*

Begin this experience by painting a powerful picture of the need for missionaries in our world.

Question #1: What is a missionary?
Ask your students: **Who are missionaries?** You will probably get a wide range of responses depending on the make-up of your group. Help your students realize that we have many perceptions of missionaries.

Now read aloud the following definition of a missionary: *A person sent out by a church/parachurch organization to preach and make converts in a foreign country.*

Have your students turn to the Book of Acts. Tell them that, together, you are going to look at "snapshots" of Paul's life. Paul was one of the first and most effective missionaries ever. Divide your students into three teams and assign each team one of the following passages: **Acts 13:13–52; Acts 14:8–28; and Acts 16:16–40.** (If you have a small D-Team group, assign each student a different passage.) Have the students look up the passages, answer the questions, and be prepared to summarize what they learned for the rest of the group.

Prep Notes

Acts 13:13–52
Who are the two missionaries in this passage? (Paul and Barnabas) *To whom were they preaching? Why?* (The Gentiles, since the Jews had already rejected their message.) *In verse 47, what did Paul say the Lord had commanded him to do?* (To bring salvation to the Gentiles.) *Would you consider Paul and Barnabas effective missionaries? Why or why not?*

Acts 14:8–28
What did Paul do that shocked the crowds in Lystra? (He healed a lame man.) *Who did the people of Lystra believe Paul and Barnabas were?* (The Greek gods Zeus and Hermes.) *What did the Jews, who were jealous of the fact that Paul was converting Gentiles, eventually do to Paul in verse 19?* (They stoned him and dragged him out of the city.)

Acts 16:16–40
What was unusual about the slave girl Paul and Silas met? (She was possessed with a spirit that allowed her to predict the future.) *Why were Paul and Silas thrown into jail?* (Paul commanded the spirit to depart from the slave girl, leaving her owners with no source of income. Paul and Silas were then accused of advocating religious customs that were unlawful for Romans to accept or practice.) *Explain what circumstances led to the release of Paul and Silas.* (An earthquake opened the jail doors. When the jailer was about to kill himself, Paul stopped him saying that the prisoners were all accounted for. Then Paul told the jailer how he could be saved.)

After your students have shared the stories of Paul's experiences, discuss the following questions: *What were some of the trials Paul faced as a missionary? What were Paul's strengths? Did you see any weaknesses?*

Remind your students that they don't have to be exactly like Paul in order to be effective missionaries. Emphasize that a missionary is anyone who is willing to devote his or her entire life to spreading the gospel. Do you have to be able to cast out spirits to be a missionary? No! Do you have to be able to sing and pray all night if you are put in jail? No! Do you have to love Jesus and want others to love Jesus? Yes!

Question #2: Why do we have missionaries?
Ask your students: *Why do we need missionaries?* Emphasize that two main reasons we need missionaries are because they are part of God's plan to spread the gospel, and because there are lost souls all over the world.

Ask your students: *Read and record your observations on the following verses: Matthew 4:17; 10:7; 11:1, 5; and Mark 13:10; 16:15.* These powerful verses will encourage your students to see that missionaries are not just something Christians created because we needed more jobs. Missionaries were created by God as a part of His plan to save the entire world.

Question #3: What do missionaries do?
Discuss the following questions with your students: *How are missionaries called to their jobs? How are missionaries paid? Are all missionaries connected with a church? How do missionaries support a family? What requirements must be met before a person can become a missionary? Is there a certain length of time missionaries must serve?*

The students should work to answer these questions; however, do not tell your students any definitive answers. These are the questions you want your students to be thinking about during the week.

REFLECTION

Your students have just learned about the who, why, and how of missionaries. Now they must figure out where they fit in. Are they cut out to be missionaries? If so, in what role and where? Hand out a piece of stationery to each one of your students. Tell them to pretend they are writing a letter to the board of a missions project. Your students must reveal why they might be interested in becoming missionaries, in what part of the world they would like to be stationed, what gifts they have, what they feel their weaknesses are, and what type of work they would be interested in doing.

Emphasize that this is a letter of self-reflection to get each of them thinking about whether or not they might be cut out for missions work. If a student says he or she already knows for sure that missions work is out of the question, have him or her write down a plan for using his or her gifts and talents to serve God without leaving the country.

Give your students a few minutes to record honest responses to the following questions, found in their Student Notes: ***What was most meaningful to you about our experience today? What does God want you to do in response?***

Ask a student to read aloud the Summary Statements in the Student Notes.

Summary Statements

We learned today that . . .
- Missionaries are people who are sent out to preach and make converts in a foreign country.
- Paul, Barnabas, and Silas are examples of the earliest and most effective missionaries.
- Missionaries are a part of God's plan.
- Missionaries are funded through churches, missions organizations, and individual donations.

MAKE AN IMPACT

. . . In Your Life
This week your students should finish reading about Paul's incredible life as a missionary. Have them start in Acts 17, where we left off today. Tell them to set a goal for themselves to try to finish reading the Book of Acts in two weeks. Remind your students to be thinking of questions to ask the missionary who will be visiting with your group next week.

. . . With Accountability
Have the D-Team members form pairs to become accountability partners for the week and to work on the memory verse. Have each student write out the **Unit Memory Verse**.

Prayer
Bring the students back together and close in prayer.

---

1. Global Messengers

Preview

As you work together through "Unit 3: Mission: Possible," you will be focusing on missions by answering three questions:

1. What are missions?
2. Why are missions important?
3. How can we support missions?

Unit Memory Verse

"For we do not preach ourselves, but Jesus Christ as Lord, and ourselves as your servants for Jesus' sake" (2 Cor. 4:5).

Focus

This week, you will discover that missions are a vital part of Christianity by answering three questions.

THE EXPERIENCE

Question #1: What is a missionary?

Who are missionaries?

Read your assigned passage, answer the questions, and be prepared to summarize what you learned for the rest of the group.

Acts 13:13–52

Who are the two missionaries in this passage? To whom were they preaching? Why?

In verse 47, what did Paul say the Lord had commanded him to do?

Summary Statements

We learned today that . . . .

- Missionaries are people who are sent out to preach and make converts in a foreign country.
- Paul, Barnabas, and Silas are examples of the earliest and most effective missionaries.
- Missionaries are a part of God's plan.
- Missionaries are funded through churches, missions organizations, and individual donations.

MAKE AN IMPACT

. . . In Your Life

Finish reading about Paul's incredible life as a missionary by starting in Acts 17, where we left off today. Set a goal for yourself to try to finish reading the Book of Acts in two weeks. Be thinking of questions to ask the missionary who will be visiting with your group next week.

. . . With Accountability

With your accountability partner, talk about your responses to the "Reflection" questions. Exchange phone numbers. Call each other this week to hold each other accountable to making an impact in your lives.

name _____ phone _____

Begin learning your memory verse by writing it in the space below.

MEMORY VERSE
2 Corinthians 4:5

Would you consider Paul and Barnabas effective missionaries? Why or why not?

Acts 14:8–28

What did Paul do that shocked the crowds in Lystra?

Who did the people of Lystra believe Paul and Barnabas were?

What did the Jews, who were jealous of the fact that Paul was converting Gentiles, eventually do to Paul in verse 19?

Acts 16:16–40

What was unusual about the slave girl Paul and Silas met?

Why were Paul and Silas thrown into jail?

Explain what circumstances led to the release of Paul and Silas.

What were some of the trials Paul faced as a missionary? What were Paul's strengths? Did you see any weaknesses?

Question #2: Why do we have missionaries?

Why do we need missionaries?

Read and record your observations on the following verses: Matthew 4:17; 10:7; 11:1, 5; and Mark 13:10; 16:15.

Question #3: What do missionaries do?

How are missionaries called to their jobs?

How are missionaries paid? Are all missionaries connected with a church?

How do missionaries support a family?

What requirements must be met before a person can become a missionary? Is there a certain length of time missionaries must serve?

REFLECTION

Pretend you are writing a letter to the board of a missions project. Reveal why you might be interested in becoming a missionary, in what part of the world you would like to be stationed, what gifts you have, what you think your weaknesses are, and what type of work you would be interested in doing. If you already know for sure that missions work is out of the question for you, write down a plan for using your gifts and talents to serve God without leaving the country.

What was most meaningful to you about our experience today?

What does God want you to do in response?

A Visit from Afar

Before the D-Team Experience

LEADER DEVOTION

As we think about missionaries, it is often difficult to know what to pray for because we have never "walked in their shoes." Read Romans 8:26–27. These verses remind us that the Spirit will lead us and let us know exactly how and for what to pray.

This D-Team experience involves a visit from a missionary. Spend time in prayer for the right person to come speak to your students. Then pray that your students will be receptive and that, if it is God's will, they might devote their lives to missions. Finally, spend time in prayer letting the Spirit lead you.

As you prepare to lead, jot down your personal experiences and insights in the "Prep Notes" column so you can share them with your students.

LOOKING AHEAD

Student Focus
During this D-Team experience, your students will learn why missions are important through two firsthand encounters:
Encounter #1: Meet a missionary.
Encounter #2: Support a missionary.

Unit Memory Verse
"For we do not preach ourselves, but Jesus Christ as Lord, and ourselves as your servants for Jesus' sake" (2 Cor. 4:5).

Practical Impact
During this D-Team experience, each student will have a firsthand experience of meeting a missionary and understanding exactly what being a missionary is all about.

BE PREPARED

Materials Needed
- Bibles, notebooks, and pens
- Duplicated Student Notes
- A missionary (or someone who has served as a missionary)
- Map (Option 1)

Special Preparation
- Contact a missionary you support or know to visit your D-Team group and share as much as possible from his or her life on the mission field. You may want to ask your students if they or their parents know of any missionaries who might be available. If you have trouble locating a missionary, check with your church board of missions, other churches in your area, or missions organizations located in your community.

- Prepare an outline of what you would like the missionary to cover with your students. Think about what your students would most like to hear and what you think they most need to hear. Make a list of questions the missionary should try to answer. If you can't arrange to meet this person prior to the D-Team experience, be sure to give him or her your list of questions via a phone conversation, mail, or fax. Use the following list of questions to supplement your own list.
    1. What was your childhood like?
    2. When did you become a Christian?
    3. When did you think you might like to be a missionary?
    4. How did you know God was calling you to be a missionary?
    5. How did you know *where* to go?
    6. How did you know *when* to go?
    7. Do you have a family?
    8. How does your family feel about your job as a missionary?
    9. What are your spiritual gifts?
    10. Describe your personality.
    11. Describe the country/city in which you are stationed.
    12. Describe the people in the country/city in which you are stationed.
    13 Describe your specific role as a missionary.
    14. Describe an average day in your life as a missionary.
    15. How do you raise support?
    16. Is raising support difficult?
    17. When were you most scared?
    18. When were you most alone?
    19. What was your biggest praise?
    20. What do you enjoy most about what you do?
    21. What do you enjoy least?
    22. What advice do you have for high school students about entering the mission field?
    23. Would you ever like to be stationed in a different part of the world?
    24. Does the world need more missionaries?
    25. Who should be a missionary?
    26. What kind of support do you most need?

Environment

To set up the environment for this D-Team experience, you can choose one of the following. Option 1 works in any setting; Option 2 moves the experience outside your normal setting.

Option 1: While the missionary is getting things set up for his or her presentation, take your students to a different part of the room. Have them think of questions and concerns they want to ask the missionary. Take some time with a map, familiarizing your students with the part of the world in which this missionary has served.

Option 2: If the missionary lives in your community, ask if you can meet at his or her house. He or she might have interesting photos, displays, or slides that would be difficult to transport.

Leading the D-Team Experience
(60 min. total)

GET STARTED

Review
Have a student read aloud the information under the "Review" in the Student Notes: *Last week, you were challenged to consider whether you were cut out to be a missionary. Share how you might use your talents to serve God.*

Student Prayer
Have a student pray for the missionary you have invited to your D-team meeting.

Focus
During this D-Team experience, your students will learn why missions are important through two firsthand encounters:

Encounter #1: Meet a missionary.
Encounter #2: Support a missionary.

THE EXPERIENCE

Have your students **read James 2:14–19.** Give your D-Team several minutes to answer the following questions: **Do you believe that if a person says he has faith but has no works, his faith will not save him? Why does it make sense that true faith will naturally be accompanied by works? Verse 18 talks about faith by works. What does this mean? What does verse 19 mean? How does this passage apply to missionaries? Do most missionaries demonstrate faith by works?**

After your students have answered the questions, take a few moments to discuss them. While most of these questions are "opinion" questions, keep the discussion focused around the idea that if we truly believe as we say we do, our actions will come naturally. The life of a missionary may seem supernatural to us, but to most of them it is second nature—just an extension of their faith. After this discussion your missionary visitor should be ready for his or her presentation.

Encounter #1: Meet a missionary.
Before your missionary visitor speaks, meet with your D-Team members and have them write out questions of their own. Encourage your students to take notes during the missionary's presentation.

Encounter #2: Support a missionary
After the missionary's presentation, your students should ask the missionary how he or she could be best supported. Encourage them to find out the biggest needs this missionary is facing. Ask each student to answer the question: **How can I support this missionary?** Then have your D-Team members form a circle around the missionary and spend time in prayer.

Prep Notes

REFLECTION

After your missionary visitor has left, find out what your students thought about the presentation. Use the following questions to debrief: **Was the missionary what you expected? Did the person demonstrate faith through his or her actions? Could you live where this person has lived? What would you struggle with as a missionary? Did this person seem to be happy/fulfilled with his or her experiences?**

Give your students a few minutes to record honest responses to the following questions, found in their Student Notes: **What was most meaningful to you about our experience today? What does God want you to do in response?**

Ask a student to read aloud the Summary Statements in the Student Notes.

Summary Statements

We learned today that . . .
- Faith without works is dead.
- Missionaries are often excellent examples of faith by works.
- The mission field is one place to which we might be called to serve.
- Missionaries are real people just like us.

MAKE AN IMPACT

. . . In Your Life
Challenge your students to spend some time thinking and praying about ways they can become active missionaries. Whether they decide to commit to go overseas, send money, or just pray, remind your students that, as Christians, we must all commit some part of our lives to building God's kingdom.

. . . With Accountability
Have the D-Team members form pairs to become accountability partners for the week and to work on the memory verse. Have each student write out the **Unit Memory Verse**.

Prayer
Bring your students back together and close with prayer.

2. A Visit from Afar

Review

Last week, you were challenged to consider whether you were cut out to be a missionary. Share how you might use your talents to serve God.

Focus

This week, you will learn why missions are important through two firsthand encounters.

THE EXPERIENCE

Read James 2:14–19. Do you believe that if a person says he has faith but has no works, his faith will not save him?

Why does it make sense that true faith will naturally be accompanied by works?

Verse 18 talks about faith by works. What does this mean?

What does verse 19 mean?

How does this passage apply to missionaries?

Summary Statements

We learned today that . . .
- Faith without works is dead.
- Missionaries are often excellent examples of faith by works.
- The mission field is one place to which we might be called to serve.
- Missionaries are real people just like us.

MAKE AN IMPACT

. . . In Your Life

Spend some time thinking and praying about ways you can become an active missionary. Whether you decide to commit to go overseas, send money, or just pray, remember that, as Christians, we must all commit some part of our lives to building God's kingdom.

. . . With Accountability

With your accountability partner, talk about your responses to the "Reflection" questions. Exchange phone numbers. Call each other this week to hold each other accountable to making an impact in your lives.

name _____ phone _____

Continue learning your memory verse by writing it in the space below and reciting it to your partner.

MEMORY VERSE
2 Corinthians 4:5

Do most missionaries demonstrate faith by works?

Encounter #1: Meet a missionary.
Before the missionary speaks, write out questions of your own. Be sure to take notes during the missionary's presentation.

Name of missionary:

Where he or she is stationed:

How many years he or she has been on the mission field:

Questions I have for the missionary:
1.

2.

3.

4.

5.

6.

Notes:

Encounter #2: Support a missionary.
After the missionary's presentation, ask the missionary how he or she could be best supported. What are the biggest needs this missionary is facing? Form a circle around the missionary and spend time in prayer.

How can I support this missionary?

REFLECTION

Was the missionary what you expected?

Did the person demonstrate faith through his or her actions?

Could you live where this person has lived?

What would you struggle with as a missionary?

Did this person seem to be happy/fulfilled with his or her experiences?

What was most meaningful to you about our experience today?

What does God want you to do in response?

Armchair Missionaries

Before the D-Team Experience

LEADER DEVOTION

This D-Team experience involves supporting a missionary with words, money, and prayer. Spend some time in prayer that your students will come to understand the importance of volunteering our money, time, and prayer to missions. Also spend time in prayer for the missionaries you know who are overseas. How are you doing in terms of the support you are willing to give? Pray for a giving spirit so that you might support the work of God's kingdom.

As you prepare to lead, jot down your personal experiences and insights in the "Prep Notes" column so you can share them with your students.

LOOKING AHEAD

Student Focus
During this D-Team experience, your students will learn how to be armchair missionaries by taking three steps:
- Step #1: Support missionaries through letters.
- Step #2: Support missionaries through offerings.
- Step #3: Support missionaries through prayers.

Unit Memory Verse
"For we do not preach ourselves, but Jesus Christ as Lord, and ourselves as your servants for Jesus' sake" (2 Cor. 4:5).

Practical Impact
During this D-Team experience, each student will have the experience of supporting a missionary through a letter, money, and prayer.

BE PREPARED

Materials Needed
- Bibles, notebooks, and pens
- Duplicated Student Notes
- A list of the names and addresses of missionaries
- Stationery, envelopes, and stamps

Special Preparation
Contact your church or area missions organization for a list of the names and addresses of missionaries. (Option 1)

Environment
To set-up the environment for this D-Team experience, you can choose one of the following. Option 1 works in any setting; Option 2 moves the experience outside your normal setting.

Option 1: Bring a list of missionaries who need to be supported either financially, through prayers, or through letters.

Option 2: Take your D-Team members to your church office, or a missionary organization in your town. Have your students ask for names and addresses of missionaries who could use financial support, prayer support, or letters of encouragement.

Leading the D-Team Experience
(60 min. total)

GET STARTED
(5 min.)

Review
Have a student read aloud the information under the "Review" in the Student Notes:
Last week, you were challenged to spend some time thinking about ways you could become a missionary. Share your insights.

Student Prayer
Ask a student to pray for giving hearts and a desire to share our resources with others.

Focus
Share with your students that during this D-Team experience, they will learn how to be armchair missionaries by taking three steps:

Step #1: Support missionaries through letters.
Step #2: Support missionaries through offerings.
Step #3: Support missionaries through prayers.

THE EXPERIENCE
(40 min.)

Step #1: Support missionaries through letters.
Ask your students: *Do you think everyone is cut out for missions?* Most of your students will give the obvious answer of no. Now ask: *Is there anything you can do to support missionaries without going abroad?* Most of your students will probably answer that they can give money.

Remind your students that there are two additional, very effective ways we can support missionaries without leaving our homes: support letters and prayers.

Before you begin the support letter, have a student *read aloud Psalm 91:4–7.* Ask: *How do these verses make you feel?* (sheltered, protected, safe, secure, taken care of). Tell your students that this is how we want to make our missionaries feel as they experience the loneliness of being so far from their homes and families.

You may approach writing a support letter in two ways. The first way is to bring in a list of missionaries and decide as a group who you will support. Or you could split up the names so that each D-Team member makes contact with a different missionary.

Once you have decided to whom your students will be writing, have your students close their eyes and ask them: *If you were a missionary on an island far away and had been there for years, what would you most like to hear in a letter?* Have your students brainstorm for a few moments. Then have them start their letters of support. Give them about twenty minutes to complete their letters. Tell them to make the letters as neat as possible. Be sure your students put the letters in the envelopes and address them. Remind your students of the comfort that comes from Scripture. Tell them to include at least one verse in their letters. Have students share these verses with each other.

Prep Notes

Ask several students to **read aloud the following verses: Luke 6:38; Acts 20:35; 1 Timothy 6:17–18; and Hebrews 13:16.** Most of your students have probably heard these verses before. Ask: **Why are we asked to give? Do you tithe regularly? Are you generous with your money? Do you currently support any missions/missionaries? Would you like to be more consistent in your giving?**

Tell your students that today we will take the first step in sharing the resources God has given us.

Step #2: Support missionaries through offerings.
Ask: **What is the best way to raise money to send to missionaries?** You might suggest that each student give the money he or she has at the moment. However, it would probably be more meaningful to take an offering now, and then plan an activity where the students will take ownership and raise money to be sent.

Step #3: Support missionaries through prayers.
The last step is to spend about ten minutes in prayer for the missionary or missionaries whom your students selected to support. Before you begin to pray, have your students **read the following Scriptures: Mark 11:24; 1 Thessalonians 5:17; Romans 12:10–13; and Philippians 1:3–6.** Ask: **Why should we pray for missionaries?** (Because if we believe, we shall receive; because we are told to pray; because we should pray not only for ourselves, but for each other; because we must support one another.)

Brainstorm with your students some of the areas in which a missionary might need prayer. Ask your students: **Remember the missionary who came to speak last week? What were some of the areas on which he or she touched?** After your students have developed a fairly detailed list, either divide up the list or have an open prayer with one person designated to close the prayer.

🕐 **(5 min.)**

REFLECTION

Share with your students that although they took an offering tonight, there is much more that they are capable of giving to the missionaries of the world. Brainstorm for a few moments about what fund-raiser your students would like to participate in. Some suggestions: a car wash, community service projects, baby-sitting. Then let the students select the fund-raiser and set the date. Delegate jobs so that this is something the students are doing. You should oversee but not coordinate. After the event, have the students count the money, write a letter explaining how they earned it, and then mail it to the missionary.

Give your students a few minutes to record honest responses to the following questions, found in their Student Notes: **What was most meaningful to you about our experience today? What does God want you to do in response?**

Ask a student to read aloud the Summary Statements in the Student Notes.

Summary Statements

We learned today that . . .
- Missionaries need to be supported through letters.
- We have been instructed to give to others.
- We must lift one another up in prayer.

MAKE AN IMPACT

10 min.)

. . . In Your Life

Challenge your students to spend time praying for the missionary to whom they wrote. If possible, they should try to gain more information about the person and the missionary organization with which he or she is associated. Encourage them to expect some return correspondence that will let them know that their letters *do* make a difference.

. . . With Accountability

Have the D-Team members form pairs to become accountability partners for the week and to work on the memory verse. Have each student write out and recite the **Unit Memory Verse** to his or her partner. Then ask each pair to share the significance of the memory verse in his or her life.

Prayer

Bring the students back together and close in prayer.

3. Armchair Missionaries

Review

Last week, you were challenged to spend some time thinking about ways you could become a missionary. Share your insights.

Focus

This week, you will learn how to be an armchair missionary by taking three steps.

THE EXPERIENCE

Step #1: Support missionaries through letters.
Do you think everyone is cut out for missions?

Is there anything you can do to support missionaries without going abroad?

Read Psalm 91:4–7. How do these verses make you feel?

If you were a missionary on an island far away and had been there for years, what would you most like to hear in a letter?

MAKE AN IMPACT

. . . In Your Life

This week, spend time praying for the missionary to whom you wrote. If possible, try to gain more information about the person and the missionary organization with which he or she is associated. Expect some return correspondence that will let you know that your letter *does* make a difference.

. . . With Accountability

With your accountability partner, talk about your responses to the "Reflection" questions. Exchange phone numbers. Call each other this week to hold each other accountable to making an impact in your lives.

name _____ phone _____

Continue learning your memory verse by writing it in the space below and reciting it to your partner. Share with your partner the significance this memory verse has for your life.

MEMORY VERSE
2 Corinthians 4:5

Read Luke 6:38; Acts 20:35; 1 Timothy 6:17–18; and Hebrews 13:16. Why are we asked to give?

Do you tithe regularly?

Are you generous with your money?

Do you currently support any missions/missionaries?

Would you like to be more consistent in your giving?

Step #2: Support missionaries through offerings.
What is the best way to raise money to send to missionaries?

Step #3: Support missionaries through prayers.
Read Mark 11:24; 1 Thessalonians 5:17; Romans 12:10–13; and Philippians 1:3–6. Why should we pray for missionaries?

Spend about ten minutes in prayer for the missionary or missionaries whom you selected to support. List some areas in which a missionary might need prayer.

Remember the missionary who came to speak last week? What were some of the areas on which he or she touched?

R E F L E C T I O N

Although we took an offering today, there is much more we are capable of giving to the missionaries of the world. Think for a few moments about what fund-raiser you would like to participate in.

What was most meaningful to you about our experience today?

What does God want you to do in response?

Summary Statements

We learned today that . . .
- Missionaries need to be supported through letters.
- We have been instructed to give to others.
- We must lift one another up in prayer.

ON A MISSION

LEADER FOCUS

This unit will involve high participation because of its service opportunities. In order for you to be prepared, focus on your own willingness to be a full participant. Take a gauge reading on your heart. Paul gave us a glimpse of Christ's example in Philippians 2:5–11. Read what he wrote regarding becoming a servant. Look to your Lord and Savior as your model!

BIG PICTURE

Unit Overview
In Unit 4 we will be focusing on how individual students can make an impact in their world in three action areas: (1) by becoming a student missionary; (2) by becoming a voice in the world; and (3) by impacting the world together.

1. Campus Connection
During this D-Team experience, your students will discover the incredible opportunities they have to be missionaries in their schools by taking three steps:

> Step #1: Understand that everyone is a missionary.
> Step #2: Determine how we should act as missionaries.
> Step #3: Establish a plan of action.

2. Voice in the World
During this D-Team experience, your students will learn how to be a voice in the world by going through two phases of preparation:

> Phase #1: Determine who to pray for.
> Phase #2: Determine how to pray for them.

3. Mission Ready
During this D-Team experience, your students will learn how to impact the world together by equipping themselves with three tools:

> Tool #1: Passport—power and protection
> Tool #2: Prayer chain
> Tool #3: Truth—the Bible

STUDENT IMPACT

Unit Memory Verse

"Live such good lives among the pagans that, though they accuse you of doing wrong, they may see your good deeds and glorify God on the day He visits us" (1 Peter 2:12).

Unit 1 Introduction

Campus Connection

Before the D-Team Experience

LEADER DEVOTION

This D-Team experience will challenge your students to be missionaries to their schools. But before you prepare to challenge *them*, take the challenge yourself. God has called all of us to be missionaries. You are called to be one in your own environment. If you work full-time in the workplace, do you see yourself as a missionary to those people? Take a moment to evaluate your answer to that question and then determine what God would want you to change to improve your missionary skills. As you prepare to lead, jot down your personal experiences and insights in the "Prep Notes" column so you can share them with your students.

LOOKING AHEAD

Student Focus
During this D-Team experience, your students will discover the incredible opportunities they have to be missionaries in their schools by taking three steps:
    Step #1: Understand that everyone is a missionary.
    Step #2: Determine how we should act as missionaries.
    Step #3: Establish a plan of action.

Unit Memory Verse
"Live such good lives among the pagans that, though they accuse you of doing wrong, they may see your good deeds and glorify God on the day He visits us" (1 Peter 2:12).

Practical Impact
During this D-Team experience, your students will be learning about being missionaries on their school campuses. They will be receiving passports into their schools that will remind them of their mission field.

BE PREPARED

Materials Needed
- Bibles, notebooks, and pens
- Duplicated Student Notes
- Atlas
- Yearbook from a local high school
- CD or cassette tape player
- A recording of "AKA Public School" by Audio Adrenaline (*Don't Censor Me*, Up In The Mix Music/BMI, 1993)

Special Preparation
    Prepare passports for your students that indicate safe passage to their local high school.

Environment

To set up the environment for this D-Team experience, you can choose one of the following. Option 1 works in any setting; Option 2 moves the experience outside your normal setting.

Option 1: Put the atlas on a table so everyone can see it. Or display a large world map on the wall.

Option 2: Plan to meet somewhere close to your students' high school, so that you could end your D-Team experience with prayer in your students' high school parking lot.

Leading the D-Team Experience
(60 min. total)

GET STARTED

(5 min.)

Unit Preview
Have a student read aloud the information under the "Preview" in the Student Notes:
As you work together through "Unit 4: On a Mission," you will be focusing on how you can make an impact in your world in three action areas:
1. *By becoming a student missionary.*
2. *By becoming a voice in the world.*
3. *By impacting the world together.*

Unit Memory Verse
Read aloud 1 Peter 2:12, "Live such good lives among the pagans that, though they accuse you of doing wrong, they may see your good deeds and glorify God on the day He visits us. "Explain that a believer's good life may influence an unbeliever to repent and believe.

Student Prayer
Ask a senior or junior to pray for your D-Team members.

Focus
Share with your D-Team members that this week, they will discover the incredible opportunities they have to be missionaries in their schools by taking three steps:

Step #1: Understand that everyone is a missionary.
Step #2: Determine how we should act as missionaries.
Step #3: Establish a plan of action.

THE EXPERIENCE

(40 min.)

Take the first ten to fifteen minutes to talk to your students about a missionary trip you would like to take with them within the next year. Get them excited about really doing this. Pull out your world atlas and, together, pick a place that they think needs their help and evangelism the most.

Take time to talk about these issues:
- Cost of the trip—How will you raise the money?
- Transportation—How will you get there?
- Message—What would you want to say to the people?
- Mode of communication—Who would communicate the message?
- Expectations—How would the people respond?
- Cultural differences—How will you manage a different language, dress, etc.?

Ask: *How would you respond if you were told that the funds have already been paid for a missionary trip to a specific place, and that the need is enormous and urgent. Are you game to go? Are you willing to put forth effort to make it happen?*

Pull out the yearbook and display it on the table. Tell your students you want them to

Prep Notes

see the "natives of the land" that need their help desperately. Turn through the pages so they see their friends' faces.

Play a recording of the song "AKA Public School" by Audio Adrenaline. Discuss how the lyrics offer them a new purpose for getting up every day and going to school.

Step #1: Understand that everyone is a missionary.
Establish that God has called all of us to be "missionaries" by having your students **read Acts 1:8.** Ask: **What does Jesus ask us to be specifically?** (He asks us to be a witness.) Emphasize that Jesus told the disciples to be witnesses in their hometowns—then to reach farther out.

Have a student **read aloud Matthew 28:19–20.** Ask: **What were Jesus' last words to us?** Note that Jesus could have said anything, but He chose to tell us to be witnesses and reach our friends with the gospel message.

Step #2: Determine how we should act as missionaries.
Explain that God is specific about how to reach our friends. Ask three students to **read 1 Corinthians 10:23–24; Philippians 2:14–16; and Colossians 3:12–17; 4:5–6.** Ask: **What does Paul say will influence our friends' decisions to check out a personal relationship with Jesus?** Summarize that our actions shouldn't cause others to stumble or turn away from Christ. We should seek the other person's best interest, which will in turn direct that person toward Christ. In addition, we should do everything without complaining or arguing so that we are blameless and pure. We should shine like stars so that others will see us. Finally, we should be compassionate, kind, humble, gentle, and patient. But above all we should have love ruling our hearts, which will in turn influence our actions.

Step #3: Establish a plan of action.
Ask: **How will today's study change the way you live your life at school and with your friends and peers? Do you have any fears or hesitations? What are they and how can you overcome them?** Encourage your students to **read Ephesians 6:10; Psalm 31:24; Hebrews 13:6; and Isaiah 41:9–10.**

Bring the discussion full circle by referring to the missionary trip your students brainstormed about in the beginning of this study. Discuss each of the issues again, but with their local high school as their foreign mission site.

Distribute passports that will get your students into the "foreign land"—their school. Talk about how it's a passport from God that gives them the authority to be bold. Also, it assures them that they will have protection during their time there. Tell them that it is their personal passport, and their time is limited—they shouldn't waste a moment of it!

 (5 min.)

REFLECTION

Open the yearbook again and have each student pick a "region"—i.e., two to three friends to whom they would personally like to focus their efforts. Have your students write their friends' names on the passport.

Give your students a few minutes to record honest responses to the following questions, found in their Student Notes: **What was most meaningful to you about our experience today? What does God want you to do in response?**

Ask a student to read aloud the Summary Statements in the Student Notes.

> **Summary Statements**
>
> We learned today that . . .
> - God has called each one of us to be His witnesses—His missionaries.
> - God gives us instructions in His word that tell us how we can reach our friends.
> - We don't have to be afraid to be missionaries to our friends—God will be our strength.

MAKE AN IMPACT

(10 min.)

. . . In Your Life
How do we begin this "missionary trip"? Challenge your students to determine two to three changes they will make this next week that will get their missionary trip started. Ask them how their lives will be different, and what might their peers notice once the "trip" begins.

. . . With Accountability
Have the D-Team members form pairs to become accountability partners for the week and to work on the memory verse. Have each student write out the **Unit Memory Verse**.

Prayer
Bring the students back together and close with prayer.

1. Campus Connection

Preview

As you work together through "Unit 4: On a Mission," you will be focusing on how you can make an impact in your world in three action areas:

1. By becoming a student missionary.
2. By becoming a voice in the world.
3. By impacting the world together.

Unit Memory Verse

"Live such good lives among the pagans that, though they accuse you of doing wrong, they may see your good deeds and glorify God on the day He visits us" (1 Peter 2:12).

Focus

This week, you will discover the incredible opportunities you have to be a missionary in your school by taking three steps.

THE EXPERIENCE

How would you respond if you were told that the funds have already been paid for a missionary trip to a specific place, and the need is enormous and urgent. Are you game to go? Are you willing to put forth effort to make it happen?

Step #1: Understand that everyone is a missionary.
Read Acts 1:8. What does Jesus ask us to be specifically?

"Reflection" questions. Exchange phone numbers. Call each other this week to hold each other accountable to making an impact in your lives.

name

phone

Begin learning your memory verse by writing it in the space below.

MEMORY VERSE
1 Peter 2:12

Read Matthew 28:19–20. What were Jesus' last words to us?

Step #2: Determine how we should act as missionaries.

God is specific about how to reach our friends. Read 1 Corinthians 10:23–24; Philippians 2:14–16; and Colossians 3:12–17, 4:5–6. What does Paul say will influence our friends' decisions to check out a personal relationship with Jesus?

1 Corinthians 10:23–24

Philippians 2:14–16

Colossians 3:12–17, 4:5–6

Step #3: Establish a plan of action.

How will today's study change the way you live your life at school and with your friends and peers?

Do you have any fears or hesitations? What are they and how can you overcome them?

For encouragement, read Ephesians 6:10; Psalm 31:24; Hebrews 13:6; Isaiah 41:9–10.

REFLECTION

Open the yearbook again and pick a "region"—two or three friends on whom you would personally like to focus your efforts. Write your friends' names on your passport.

What was most meaningful to you about our experience today?

What does God want you to do in response?

Summary Statements

We learned today that . . .

- God has called each one of us to be His witnesses—His missionaries.
- God gives us instructions in His word that tell us how we can reach our friends.
- We don't have to be afraid to be missionaries to our friends—God will be our strength.

MAKE AN IMPACT

. . . In Your Life

How do we begin this "missionary trip"? Try to determine two or three changes you will make this next week that will get your missionary trip started. How will your life be different? What will your peers notice once the "trip" begins?

. . . With Accountability

With your accountability partner, talk about your responses to the

Voice in the World

Before the D-Team Experience

LEADER DEVOTION

"The prayer of the feeblest saint on earth who lives in the Spirit and keeps right with God is a terror to Satan. The very powers of darkness are paralyzed by prayer; no spiritual seance can succeed in the presence of a humble praying saint. No wonder Satan tries to keep our minds fussy in active work till we cannot think in prayer" (Oswald Chambers, *Draper's Book of Quotations for the Christian World,* Tyndale, 494).

In preparation for this D-Team experience, spend some time in prayer for your students and the lesson they will learn. As you prepare to lead, jot down your personal experiences and insights in the "Prep Notes" column so you can share them with your students.

LOOKING AHEAD

Student Focus

During this D-Team experience, your students will learn how to be a voice in the world by going through two phases of preparation:

    Phase #1: Determine who to pray for.

    Phase #2: Determine how to pray for them.

Unit Memory Verse

"Live such good lives among the pagans that, though they accuse you of doing wrong, they may see your good deeds and glorify God on the day He visits us" (1 Peter 2:12).

Practical Impact

Your students will be making a prayer chain out of beads that will serve as a reminder of who to pray for and how to pray for them.

BE PREPARED

Materials Needed

- Bibles, notebooks, and pens
- Duplicated Student Notes
- Beads (at least 15–20 per student) of different colors and shapes—the holes must fit over the leather strip
- Leather strips to make a bead chain or necklace—each approximately 12–16 inches long (found at craft stores)
- Newspapers—local, state, and world
- CD or tape player, quiet music

Special Preparation

- Make up envelopes or sandwich bags with leather strips and beads for each student.

• Select some quiet music. (Option 1)

Environment
To set up the environment for this D-Team experience, you can choose one of the following. Option 1 works in any setting; Option 2 moves the experience outside your normal setting.

Option 1: Create an atmosphere of prayer and worship by having praise music playing softly in the background and maybe only soft lighting—like a lamp or two—in the room.

Option 2: Weather permitting, meet outside a government building or your city hall.

Leading the D-Team Experience
(60 min. total)

GET STARTED

(5 min.)

Review
Have a student read aloud the information under the "Review" in the Student Notes:
Last week, you talked about becoming missionaries at your school. You were challenged to determine two or three changes you would make the next week that would get your missionary trip started. How was your life different because of it? Did your peers notice any difference?

Student Prayer
Ask a student to pray for God's blessing on what will take place today.

Focus
During this D-Team experience, your students will learn how to be a voice in the world by going through two phases of preparation:

Phase #1: Determine who to pray for.
Phase #2: Determine how to pray for them.

THE EXPERIENCE

(40 min.)

Begin this D-Team experience by freeing your students of any distractions. Allow five minutes of just catching up on how everyone is doing. After everyone has a chance to share, ask them to concentrate on what they will be learning today.

Distribute a bead and leather packet to each student. Explain to your students that today they will learn how to actively play a part in changing lives around the world by participating in daily prayer for key people.

Phase #1: Determine who to pray for.
For the next ten to fifteen minutes, have your students compile a list of ten to fifteen different people from around the world for whom they can pray daily. Supplement the following list with your own ideas:
1. Pastor and youth pastor
2. Leaders in your church
3. The President of the United States
4. Political leaders—local, state, and national
5. Christian friends and families
6. Fellow Christians around the world
7. Churches around the world
8. Missionaries supported by your church
9. Other missionaries around the world
10. Non-believing friends
11. Nonbelievers around the world

Have your students designate a bead for each person and string it on their leather strip. Suggest that they record the person's name and the bead color for that person in the space provided in their Student Notes.

Prep Notes

Pass out newspapers and ask your students to quickly find the latest big headlines. Then together make a list of key people for whom your students could be praying. The issues may seem prominent, but there are always people behind the headlines.

For each key person in the major news stories, ask them if they think they would be able to pray for the person involved in this situation? At this time, instruct your students to designate a bead to represent any "headline news person" prayer request and string it on their leather strip. Again, suggest that they record the person's name and the bead color for that person in the space provided in their Student Notes.

Phase #2: Determine how to pray for them.
Have your students put aside their bead project and open their Bibles to *Colossians 1:9–11.* Have a student read aloud these verses. Ask: *What example does Paul set for us?* (We should devote ourselves to prayer and ask God to open a door for the message of Christ to be communicated clearly.)

Have your students take a look at *Ephesians 6:18–20.* Ask: *How did Paul ask the Ephesians to pray?* (He instructed them to pray in the Spirit, on all occasions, with all kinds of prayers and requests.) *Based on this passage, who should we always pray for?* (We should always pray for the saints.) *What personal prayer did Paul request?* (Paul asked that he be given words so he could fearlessly make known the mystery of the gospel.)

Have a student *read aloud James 5:13–16.* Ask: *What can we learn about prayer in this passage?* (The prayer of a righteous man is powerful and effective. When someone is sick, or in trouble, or has sinned—pray for them.)

Ask your students how these passages help us determine how to pray for the ten to fifteen people we have beads for. Acknowledge that, for a number of different reasons, some of the people on their chains may be hard for you to pray for. Maybe the students don't know them, or they don't like what they represent or support. Remind your students that every single person matters to God. It doesn't matter who they are or what their jobs are or what they may have done. All are the same in God's eyes, and all need prayer. It's very important that the students know that their prayers could make the difference in that person's eternity.

Suggest the following ways of praying for others:
- Ask God to bless that person or persons today in a special way.
- Ask God to bring another believer into that person's life to minister to him or her.
- Ask God to open the person's eyes to a need for a Savior in his or her life.

 (5 min.)

REFLECTION

Have your students spend some time praying for these people. You could ask them to pair up or break into groups of three. Encourage everyone to participate in the prayer time.

Before you actually break to pray, take a moment to explain that the prayer beads are only to serve as a reminder that these people around the world need our prayers too. It is simply a way of encouraging your students to be in prayer for their world. They don't have to pray in any certain order or with any set prayers.

Now, allow your students to bring these people from around the world to the throne of God, where they will find grace, forgiveness, and comfort.

Give your students a few minutes to record honest responses to the following questions, found in their Student Notes: **What was most meaningful to you about our experience today? What does God want you to do in response?**

Ask a student to read aloud the Summary Statements in the Student Notes.

Summary Statements

We learned today that . . .
- We can make an impact in our world by praying for others around the world.
- No matter who the person is, he or she matters to God and needs prayer.
- We can always pray for a person—for God's blessing or for that person to come to know the Lord.

MAKE AN IMPACT

(10 min.)

. . . In Your Life
Challenge your students to commit to praying ten minutes daily for the people on their prayer bead chain. Instruct them to either wear the chain, or hang it somewhere that will be noticeable daily—their mirror, night stand, dresser, or car rearview mirror.

. . . With Accountability
Have the D-Team members form pairs to become accountability partners for the week and to work on the memory verse. Have each student write out the **Unit Memory Verse**.

Prayer
Bring the students back together and close in prayer.

2. Voice in the World

Review
Last week, you talked about becoming missionaries at your school. You were challenged to determine two or three changes you would make the next week that would get your missionary trip started. How was your life different because of it? Did your peers notice any difference?

Focus
This week, you will learn how to be a voice in the world by going through two phases of preparation.

THE EXPERIENCE

Try to free yourself of any distractions before concentrating on what you will be learning today.

Phase #1: Determine who to pray for.
For the next ten to fifteen minutes, compile a list of ten to fifteen different people from around the world for whom you can pray daily. Designate a bead for each person and string it on your leather strip. Record the bead's color and the person's name below.

Pastor and youth pastor
Name: _____   Bead color: _____

Leaders in your church
Name: _____   Bead color: _____

The President of the United States
Name: _____   Bead color: _____

Political leaders—local, state, and national
Name: _____   Bead color: _____
Name: _____   Bead color: _____
Name: _____   Bead color: _____

Summary Statements
We learned today that . . .
- We can make an impact in our world by praying for others around the world.
- No matter who the person is, he or she matters to God and needs prayer.
- We can always pray for a person—for God's blessing or for that person to come to know the Lord.

MAKE AN IMPACT

. . . In Your Life
Try to commit to ten minutes a day in prayer for the people on your prayer bead chain. Either wear the chain, or hang it somewhere that will be noticeable daily—on your mirror, night stand, dresser, or car rearview mirror.

. . . With Accountability
With your accountability partner, talk about your responses to the "Reflection" questions. Exchange phone numbers. Call each other this week to hold each other accountable to making an impact in your lives.

name _____   phone _____

Continue learning your memory verse by writing it in the space below and reciting it to your partner.

MEMORY VERSE
1 Peter 2:12

Christian friends and families
Name: Bead color:
Name: Bead color:

Fellow Christians around the world
Name: Bead color:
Name: Bead color:

Churches around the world
Name: Bead color:

Missionaries supported by your church
Name: Bead color:
Name: Bead color:

Other missionaries around the world
Name: Bead color:

Non-believing friends
Name: Bead color:

Nonbelievers around the world
Name: Bead color:

Quickly browse through the newspapers and find the latest big headlines. Then make a list of key people for whom you could be praying.

1.

2.

3.

4.

Designate a bead to represent any "headline news person" prayer request and string it on your leather strip.

Bead color 1:
Bead color 2:
Bead color 3:
Bead color 4:

Phase #2: Determine how to pray for them.

Read Colossians 1:9–11. What example does Paul set for us?

Read Ephesians 6:18–20. How did Paul ask the Ephesians to pray?

Based on this passage, who should we always pray for?

What personal prayer did Paul request?

Read James 5:13–16. What can we learn about prayer in this passage?

REFLECTION

Spend some time praying for these people. Your prayer beads will serve as a reminder that these people around the world need our prayers too. It is simply a way of encouraging you to be in prayer for their world. You don't have to pray in any certain order or with any set prayers.

What was most meaningful to you about our experience today?

What does God want you to do in response?

Mission Ready

3

Before the D-Team Experience

LEADER DEVOTION

Dear Leader,

As you come to Me, the living Stone—rejected by men but chosen by God and precious to Him—you also, like living stones, are being built into a spiritual house to be a holy priesthood, offering spiritual sacrifices acceptable to God through Me.

But you are a chosen person, a royal priesthood, an holy nation, a person belonging to God, that you may declare My praises. I called you out of darkness into My wonderful light. Once you were not My child, but now you are a child of Mine; once you had not received mercy, but now you have received mercy.

All authority in heaven and on earth has been given to Me. Therefore, (your name), go and make disciples of all nations, baptizing them in the name of the Father and of the Son and of the Holy Spirit, and teaching them to obey everything I have commanded you. And surely I am with you always, to the very end of the age.

I love you my child,
Jesus

As you prepare to lead, jot down your personal experiences and insights in the "Prep Notes" column so you can share them with your students.

LOOKING AHEAD

Student Focus
During this D-Team experience, your students will learn how to impact the world together by equipping themselves with three tools:
Tool #1: Passport—power and protection
Tool #2: Prayer chain
Tool #3: Truth—the Bible

Unit Memory Verse
"Live such good lives among the pagans that, though they accuse you of doing wrong, they may see your good deeds and glorify God on the day He visits us" (1 Peter 2:12).

Practical Impact
During this D-Team experience, there will be a commissioning ceremony for those students who would like to make a difference in their world through Jesus Christ. They will receive their orders and take with them their tools to aid them.

Materials Needed
- Bibles, notebooks, and pens
- Duplicated Student Notes
- Tape or chalk
- A sealed letter (containing "orders") addressed to each student

Special Preparation
- Draw a line with chalk (or tape) that divides your meeting room.
- Write a letter to each student with the following words:

Dear (*student's name*),

As you come to Me, the living Stone—rejected by men but chosen by God and precious to Him—you also, like living stones, are being built into a spiritual house to be a holy priesthood, offering spiritual sacrifices acceptable to God through Me.

But you are a chosen person, a royal priesthood, an holy nation, a person belonging to God, that you may declare My praises. I called you out of darkness into My wonderful light. Once you were not My child, but now you are a child of Mine; once you had not received mercy, but now you have received mercy.

All authority in heaven and on earth has been given to Me. Therefore, (your name), go and make disciples of all nations, baptizing them in the name of the Father and of the Son and of the Holy Spirit, and teaching them to obey everything I have commanded you. And surely I am with you always, to the very end of the age.

I love you my child,
　　　　　Jesus

Put the letter in an envelope and seal it. It should look as professional as possible. If you don't have good handwriting, then type the letters or ask someone else to write them for you.

- Inform your D-Team members ahead of time to come dressed up a little more in order to give a greater degree of importance to what will happen today. They also need to bring their passport and their prayer bead chain with them.
- Spend a good deal of time praying for your students and the impact that this D-Team experience will have on them. If there are students who are not ready for today's challenge, then encourage them to relax and observe. Allow them to ask questions of you or your students, but don't allow their presence to dictate or water down what you will do today.

Environment
To set up the environment for this D-Team experience, you can choose one of the following. Option 1 works in any setting; Option 2 moves the experience outside your normal setting.

Option 1: Draw a line with chalk (or tape) that divides your meeting room so that your students can cross and make a statement with it. Make it a celebration/ceremony atmosphere similar to a graduation ceremony or party. Ask your students to dress up a little more for this experience.

Option 2: Try meeting within a classroom or in your church somewhere. Your students should feel as though they are taking a step from the classroom, where they learn things, out into the world, where they will apply what they have learned. Again, draw a line with chalk (or tape) that divides your meeting room so that your students can cross and make a statement with it.

Leading the D-Team Experience
(60 min. total)

GET STARTED

Review
Have a student read aloud the information under the "Review" in the Student Notes: *Last week, you were challenged to pray every day for ten minutes. How did you do with that challenge? Did you do it every day?*

Student Prayer
Ask one of your key students to pray for God's blessing on what will take place today.

Focus
Share with your D-Team members that this week they will learn how to impact the world together by equipping themselves with three tools:

Tool #1: Passport—power and protection
Tool #2: Prayer chain
Tool #3: Truth—the Bible

THE EXPERIENCE

Begin this experience by explaining that we will be briefly reviewing the last two experiences. This will help prepare them for the commissioning ceremony.

Remind your students that throughout this unit we have been asking ourselves what we personally can do to make an impact on the world. Your students have been given tools to take with them that will serve them throughout the duration of their service. Now, just because the students have these tools doesn't mean they are finished learning and have all the answers. The tools are called tools because they are an assistant to what Christ will do through them. As with all tools, they must be maintained and sharpened periodically. And sometimes they will learn a different way to use a tool.

Tool #1: Passport—power and protection
Two weeks ago, your students received a passport. Ask: *Do you remember the purpose of the passport you received two weeks ago? What is it supposed to remind you of?* (It was to remind them that they are called to be missionaries to those around them—friends at school, etc. It also was a reminder that God would give them power and provide protection when they were out on the mission field.) Ask your students if they have their passports with them today. If so, have them put them out where they can see them.

Tool #2: Prayer chain
Last week your students made a prayer chain with different colored beads. Each bead represented different people and prayer requests. Ask your students if they remember what each of the beads represents. See if they have been able to use the chain and how it has served them in their prayer lives. Say: *Last week you made a prayer chain with different colored beads. How has the prayer chain given you a different perspective on the people you have been praying for?* If they brought their chain, ask them to display that also right now.

Tool #3: Truth—the Bible

Ask your students to take out their Bibles and turn to **Hebrews 4:12.** After a student reads aloud the verse, ask: **What can we learn about God's Word from this verse?** (It is quick and powerful and sharper than any two-edged sword.)

Have your students **read Psalm 119:105.** Ask: **What can we learn about God's Word from this verse?** (The Word sheds light on the dark areas of our lives.)

Ask a student to **read aloud Timothy 3:16–17.** Ask: **What can we learn about God's Word from this verse?** (God's Word is useful for teaching and training, and it is how we are equipped to do good works.)

🕐 **(15 min.)**

R E F L E C T I O N

Now ask your students to stand and form a line side-by-side, facing the chalk line on the floor. Instruct them to hold their passports, their prayer chains, and their Bibles for the commissioning and the giving of the orders.

Ask each individual student to respond to the following questions:

1. Are you equipped with all the tools necessary to impact the world around you?

2. If so, are you ready to take a step across the line in front of you as a symbol of your desire to be used by God in whatever way He sees fit to use you?

3. Do you feel you are ready to say anything, go anywhere, do whatever task needs to be done in order for the gospel to be heard by every creature? If so, take a step across the line and get ready for your mission.

As each student steps across, shake his or her hand or give a hug of affirmation. Tell each one that he or she is commissioned to go and be Jesus' witness.

Continue until everyone has been asked all of the questions and has crossed the line. After they are all on the other side, inform them that they have their first set of "orders" directly from the King, and then hand out the sealed letters you prepared. Allow a moment for them to read the letters. Then tell them to put the letter in their Bibles as a reminder of their commission.

Remind your students that just because they have taken the step they took today doesn't mean they have "arrived with all the answers." They need to continually be sharpening their tools within the walls of the body of Christ.

Give your students a few minutes to record honest responses to the following questions, found in their Student Notes: **What was most meaningful to you about our experience today? What does God want you to do in response?**

Ask a student to read aloud the Summary Statements in the Student Notes.

Summary Statements

We learned today that . . .
- Three critical tools will equip us to bring the Gospel of Jesus to our world.
- These tools are first, our passport of power and protection; second, prayer; and third, truth—God's Word.
- We are commissioned to be Christ's witnesses to the world.

MAKE AN IMPACT

. . . In Your Life
Challenge your students to make time to use each of their three tools on a daily basis. What will they need to change in order to see that realistically happen? What will be noticeably different because of today's decision? Suggest that your students contact two or three of their friends who they listed on the back of their passports and take the next step in sharing Christ with them.

. . . With Accountability
Have the D-Team members form pairs to become accountability partners for the week and to work on the memory verse. Have each student write out and recite the **Unit Memory Verse** to his or her partner. Then ask each pair to share the significance of the memory verse in his or her life.

Prayer
Bring the students back together and close in prayer.

3. Mission Ready

Review

Last week, you were challenged to pray every day for ten minutes. How did you do with that challenge? Did you do it every day?

Focus

This week, you will learn how to impact the world together by equipping yourself with three tools.

THE EXPERIENCE

Tool #1: Passport—power and protection

Do you remember the purpose of the passport you received two weeks ago? What is it supposed to remind you of?

Tool #2: Prayer chain

Last week you made a prayer chain with different colored beads. Do you remember what each of the beads represents?

How has the prayer chain given you a different perspective on the people for whom you have been praying?

Continue learning your memory verse by writing it in the space below and reciting it to your partner. Share with your partner the significance this memory verse has for your life.

MEMORY VERSE
1 Peter 2:12

Tool #3: Truth—the Bible

Read Hebrews 4:12. What can we learn about God's Word from this verse?

Read Psalm 119:105. What can we learn about God's Word from this verse?

Read Timothy 3:16–17. What can we learn about God's Word from this verse?

REFLECTION

Now stand and form a line side-by-side, facing the chalk line on the floor. You will need your passport, your prayer chain, and your Bible for the commissioning and the giving of the orders.

What was most meaningful to you about our experience today?

What does God want you to do in response?

Summary Statements

We learned today that . . .

- Three critical tools will equip us to bring the Gospel of Jesus to our world.
- These tools are first, our passport of power and protection; second, prayer; and third, truth—God's Word.
- We have been commissioned to be Christ's witnesses to the world.

MAKE AN IMPACT

. . . In Your Life

Try to make time to use each of your three tools on a daily basis. What do you need to change in order to see that realistically happen?

What will be noticeably different because of today's decision?

Contact two or three of your friends who you listed on the back of your passport and take the next step in sharing with them about Christ.

. . . With Accountability

With your accountability partner, talk about your responses to the "Reflection" questions. Exchange phone numbers. Call each other this week to hold each other accountable to making an impact in your lives.

name	phone

Shepherding Summary Form

Complete this form immediately after every meeting and give a copy to your ministry director or small groups coordinator.

ATTENDANCE

Leader:

Apprentice leader:

Members present: Guests filling the "empty chair":

Members absent:

                                                Starting core number:

ACTIVITY SUMMARY

Briefly describe how you incorporated the CLEAR values listed below.

Christ—How was Christ made the central focus of your time together?

Listen— Were you able to meet the students' needs to be heard? What concerns arose?

Empty chair—Are students praying for specific friends they could invite to join the small group? How are you fostering an openness to new members?

Affirm—In what ways were you able to affirm your students?

Read and pray—How effective was your time in the Word and in prayer together?

CELEBRATION

What's happening in your small group that you'd like to celebrate or note? What problems or questions do you need help with?

WILLOW CREEK

RESOURCES

This resource was created to serve you.

It is just one of many ministry tools that are part of the Willow Creek Resources® line, published by the Willow Creek Association together with Zondervan Publishing House. The Willow Creek Association was created in 1992 to serve a rapidly growing number of churches from all across the denominational spectrum that are committed to helping unchurched people become fully devoted followers of Christ. There are now more than 2,500 WCA member churches worldwide.

The Willow Creek Association links like-minded leaders with each other and with strategic vision, information, and resources in order to build prevailing churches. Here are some of the ways it does that:

- **Church Leadership Conferences**—3 1/2 -day events, held at Willow Creek Community Church in South Barrington, IL, that are being used by God to help church leaders find new and innovative ways to build prevailing churches that reach unchurched people.

- **The Leadership Summit**—a once-a-year event designed to increase the leadership effectiveness of pastors, ministry staff, volunteer church leaders, and Christians in business.

- **Willow Creek Resources®**—to provide churches with a trusted channel of ministry resources in areas of leadership, evangelism, spiritual gifts, small groups, drama, contemporary music, and more. For more information, call Willow Creek Resources® at 800/876-7335. Outside the US call 610/532-1249.

- *WCA News*—a bimonthly newsletter to inform you of the latest trends, resources, and information on WCA events from around the world.

- *The Exchange*—our classified ads publication to assist churches in recruiting key staff for ministry positions.

- **The Church Associates Directory**—to keep you in touch with other WCA member churches around the world.

- *WillowNet*—an Internet service that provides access to hundreds of Willow Creek messages, drama scripts, songs, videos and multimedia suggestions. The system allows users to sort through these elements and download them for a fee.

- *Defining Moments*—a monthly audio journal for church leaders, in which Lee Strobel asks Bill Hybels and other Christian leaders probing questions to help you discover biblical principles and transferable strategies to help maximize your church's potential.

For conference and membership information please write or call:

Willow Creek Association
P.O. Box 3188
Barrington, IL 60011-3188
ph: (847) 765-0070
fax: (847) 765-5046
www.willowcreek.org

0597